ANGIE SMITH, PhD

into the deep

Finding Relief from Pressure, Exhaustion, and the Need to Perform in a Shallow World

TYNDALE MOMENTUM™

A Tyndale nonfiction imprint

Visit Tyndale online at tyndale.com.

Visit the author online at angiesmithministries.com.

Into the Deep: Finding Relief from Pressure, Exhaustion, and the Need to Perform in a Shallow World

Cover design by Libby Dykstra

Interior design by Brandi Davis

Edited by Stephanie Rische

Published in association with Yates & Yates (yates2.com).

Library of Congress Cataloging-in-Publication Data

A catalog record for this book is available from the Library of Congress.

ISBN 979-8-4005-1343-5

Printed in the United States of America

32 31 30 29 28 27 26
7 6 5 4 3 2 1

Angie Smith does it again with *Into the Deep*—we are drawn in by her humor and honesty, changed by her teaching and wisdom, and challenged by her bravery and encouragement.

ANNIE F. DOWNS
New York Times bestselling author of *That Sounds Fun*

Into the Deep is a warm and insightful call to come out of hiding. With vulnerability and hope, my friend Angie reminds us that while the world rewards shallow striving, true freedom and authenticity are found in trusting the Savior who meets us in the deep places of our lives. It's a must-read!

LYSA TERKEURST
#1 *New York Times* bestselling author and president of Proverbs 31 Ministries

Honest, holy, and hilarious, Angie Smith, with blazingly fresh insights, a PhD in psychology, and a hard-won doctorate in the school of hard knocks and real life, writes lines that are lifelines for the really exhausted among us—the ones who keep trying to live a deep life with surface-level tools and then wonder why we feel like we're drowning—but in a really shallow world. *Into the Deep* exposes all kinds of anxiety-producing, performance scripts—perfectionism, impostor syndrome, comparison—and then hands you the relief of something real and durable: a fresh way to deeply live, freely trusting that Jesus is in the depths with you.

ANN VOSKAMP
New York Times bestselling author of *One Thousand Gifts* and *WayMaker*

For Dad, who taught me to appreciate every moonshadow.

Contents

INTRODUCTION

The Deep Is Calling

Most of our days are spent being everything to everyone, managing obligations, and facing the pressures of a world that's moving faster than our minds and hearts. It's relentless, and somewhere along the way, we've settled for living a shallow life because it keeps our heads above water.

We are exhausted.

We've learned to survive, and in the process, we've given up on being transformed. We can't name it, but we feel it. I say *we* because I walk beside you in this struggle. I feel it every day, and despite praying, reading my Bible, and doing all the other things "good Christians" do, I long for an answer to the nagging question: Why is life this hard?

Here's the thing: We know we're too busy. We know it's hard to be vulnerable sometimes and social media is not always our cheerleader. We know we hate feeling left out and we feel like we have to be constantly vigilant or life will fall apart.

We've used shallow tactics. We schedule fewer activities. We remember that what we see of other people's lives isn't the whole story. I could go on and on, but you get the drift: These things aren't working.

The reason you stay busy may be different from why I stay busy. The way you feel when you're ignored may sting in ways it doesn't for me. Being reprimanded for missing a deadline or being late may bring up memories for you that I will never know. The thing is, there's no one-size-fits-all solution, even though most of what we hear tells us there's a simple formula that works for everyone.

This book is different. It is just for you—for your unique experience of the world around you, your heart, and your relationship with Jesus.

If you feel like you're just trying to survive, it's because you are. You've been doing it since the day you were born, and it has served you well in many ways. As you grew older and wiser, you figured out coping mechanisms and responses that helped you fit in and earn love—you found out that being funny or smart got you what you needed from others. Those ruts are deep, and they don't disappear because you've blown out a few more birthday candles.

I think most of us can answer the question of why life is hard. Dang it all, Eve, it was fruit.

Fruit.

We live in a fallen world, where sin invades like the snake did so many years ago. He is ruthless, that guy. But take heart, dear one. God has overcome, and we can live deeply in that truth.

That said, it isn't easy. But I think it can be easier.

The reality is that if we don't understand the deep currents of our own lives and fail to acknowledge the relentless tides that seek to disorient us, we can't truly heal. This isn't about trying harder—I think we can agree that it isn't a lack of trying that has put us in this position. This isn't a self-help, touchy-feely, bullet-point approach, because you've tried that, and you know as well as I do that it doesn't work.

Knowing that you feel a certain way isn't the same as knowing *why* you feel that way. That kind of healing only comes in the deep.

Now listen, I see how this analogy could make you nervous. I mean, I'm aware of the fact that the idea of drowning is less than appealing. What you don't know from the shore is that what you thought was most dangerous is where the Lord meets you in the most significant way. It's where you stop relying on the world to satisfy you and meet the God who rules the depths you can't survive on your own.

Don't worry—we're going to get there gradually. I'm going to ease you in, and along the way, you'll get to know a little more about the journey I went on to get here, and you'll meet some people you may have heard of but maybe never heard *from*. Trust me, the shallow life didn't show up at the turn of a century or the advent of a certain invention. It has been alive and well as long as humanity itself, and God, in His kindness, has given us examples of those who came before us but swam the same seas.

I want to ease your mind from the very beginning, because I know the intense concern that's nagging at you, and no, I won't keep using cheesy water language until you want to pull your hair out. Bear with me for a little bit, and I'll give you a rest once you've gotten a lay of the land (or water, as the case may be).

We'll start on the shoreline, where we identify the issue. We'll move to the shallows, where we consider how and why we approach the world the way we do, and finally, we'll get to the deep, where true, lasting peace and healing come.

For the record, you couldn't pay me to scuba dive. I snorkeled on my honeymoon because that's what a carefree newlywed does in the bathing suit that will never fit her again. I enjoyed it long enough to get the obligatory "cute peace sign" photo and then realized the enormous, tire-like apparatus making me look deranged was not, in fact, on my bucket list.

You wouldn't know it from the pictures, though, and I guess that's kind of the point. What looked to everyone else like a happy adventure was me pretending to enjoy the experience I was not actually enjoying.

If you've been there, friend, you've come to the right place.

I pray that by the time you close this book you will have an encounter with the God who created you to be like no one else and that you'll learn more about yourself and Him in the process.

May I pray for you before we start? That was rhetorical. I'm the boss of the words here.

Lord Jesus, only You know the aches and deep joys
of the person holding this book, and I pray they

learn that You are holding them. Please give them insight into their lives so they might become better friends, sisters, daughters, and warriors for Your Kingdom. Cover them with inexplicable peace as their pens touch paper and as they explore places in their souls they may have never touched before. Create in them a new heart that finds purpose, identity, and hope in You in ways that are fresh and remarkable. Only You, Father. This is only for You. May the meditations of our hearts and the words of our mouths honor You, and may our lives reflect Your great mercy. We commit these days ahead to You, and we thank You even before we see the fruit that will come from this time together. Guide us, Lord, and help us follow. I pray in the mighty, holy, and incomparable name of Jesus. Amen.

1

Taking Off the Mask

You are loved.

The exaggerated esteem in which my lifework is held makes me very ill at ease. I feel compelled to think of myself as an involuntary swindler.

ALBERT EINSTEIN

I've spent a good bit of my life performing in front of large audiences, and I always assumed the pressure to perform came because there were so many people watching. It turns out I was wrong.

I teach middle school English at a tiny Christian school, and this is the first year I haven't felt like I'm going to throw up when the bell rings and I head to class. It probably sounds ridiculous, but the reality is that I still feel like I'm trying to prove I know what I'm doing.

If this is how I am in front of children, I'm sure you can imagine what it feels like when I'm with other adults. I live in a constant state of *Am I proving that I can be what you need me to be?* The image I project changes based on who I'm with and the context of our interaction. Please don't laugh when

I tell you that my daughters and I argue over who has to get the pizza from the delivery guy.

It doesn't matter how small the scenario is; I feel like I'm constantly working to ensure that my interactions are smooth and I can walk away feeling like I did what was required of me to make that happen. Social events are hard for me because they mean I have to be a chameleon, and there are only so many times you can change your colors before you forget who you really are. The truth is, pretending is driven by something we might not associate it with: fear.

Here's my underlying fear in all these situations: *If they knew the real me—with all my insecurities, mistakes, and imperfections—they wouldn't love me anymore.* Every time we succeed while wearing a mask, it reinforces the lie that we're only lovable when we're performing.

That cycle is brutal, and I have a feeling you know what I'm talking about. The more we convince people we are who we don't believe we are, the higher the stakes are next time. We pretend to be someone we aren't and then shoulder the burden that comes with keeping up the scam.

What nobody talks about is how exhausting this performance becomes. When you're constantly monitoring your words, your facial expressions, and your reactions to make sure they align with the persona you've created, your nervous system never gets to rest. You're always on, always calculating how to respond in character rather than simply responding as yourself.

We're swindlers, every one of us. It's just that sometimes we don't know the cause of the pressure and insecurity that hover over us in our daily lives. The way we internally monitor how our faces are responding to others or the way we speak a curated version of what we want to say when it might paint us in a better light. And the irony of all ironies is that we walk around assuming that no one else we're talking to is doing the same.

Just out of curiosity . . . have you ever felt like you weren't smart enough? Like you had to pretend to be more intelligent than you are? I ask because I kick-started this chapter with an amazing quote about someone feeling like an "involuntary swindler." He felt like he wasn't actually that brilliant and he was confused about why there was so much hubbub about him.

In case you didn't catch it, these words were said by none other than Albert Einstein. I mean, it's a name that's synonymous with genius (well, that and #hairgoalz), and he felt like he was better at tricking people than he was with scientific formulas.

What Would Happen If They Knew?

While not officially a diagnosis, *impostor syndrome* is considered a true diagnostic issue. It isn't just a cute thing to say—it has serious implications for our mental and physical health. Where did that term come from? Glad you asked.

There were two high-achieving graduate school students who coined the term in 1978 and have studied the phenomenon for decades.[1] They aren't the only ones, and as you might imagine, the field has exploded with the advent of social media and all the other fun ways we feel pressure to keep up whatever version of ourselves we've persuaded people to believe is real.

I have to tell you this wacky story I heard about years ago because it definitely wins the superlative for "least likely to give up the scam." His name was Chung Ling Soo, and he was an Asian magician who gained notoriety for his quirkiness. First of all, he didn't speak onstage. Ever. Which was mostly because he was really an American born as William Robinson. Turns out he had been unsuccessful until his manager told him that Asian magicians were in demand. At this point, he shaved his head, bought some makeup, and took his kind-of wife (that's a story for another day) on a freaky road show. And he pulled it off until one night when he didn't.

On March 23, 1918, he took his place onstage the way he had for years and held a bullet under his tongue. His assistant fired a rigged gun, and before he could move the bullet to the front of his mouth to make it appear he had caught it with his teeth, tragedy struck. There was too much gunpowder in the rigged gun, causing a real bullet to shoot out and pierce him through the lung. As he realized what had happened, he gasped and said the only words he would ever utter onstage: "Oh my God—something's happened. Lower the curtain."

I'm going on record as saying the curtain would not even be part of my first few hundred thoughts. Also, I feel like the whole "Something has happened" thing was kind of a given at that point, but kudos to him for clarifying. I don't know how many budding magicians were in the audience, but I'm guessing they took a follow-up StrengthsFinder quiz immediately.

I mean, y'all. The guy knows he's about to die, and in that moment, what he is most concerned with is maintaining the act.

Close the curtain.

The first words he ever spoke onstage and the last breaths he took in this life were directed toward an audience of strangers he didn't want to know the truth. *I am not who you think I am, and I would rather die than have you realize it.* Extreme, yes. But it's not that hard to draw comparisons to our own lives.

What would happen if they knew?

When Your False Self Lets You Down

Here's the spiritual wound at the core of all pretending: We believe the lie that love is conditional and based on our performance. We think we have to earn love—from God and from others—by being perfect, successful, funny, helpful, or whatever role we learned would keep us safe. But this belief cuts us off from the very love we're desperately seeking.

We all have false selves, and they have served us well in the past.

The problem is that they don't serve us well for the long haul, but because we have hidden behind them for so long, it's hard to stop the charade.

Eventually we don't even know where the line is between who we are and who we are pretending to be.

I love the way author David Benner says it: "We do not find our true self by seeking it. Rather, we find it by seeking

God."[2] I don't know David Benner, but I plan to find him in heaven and tell him how much his work has meant to me. In fact, I considered just stapling his pages here instead of mine (that just autocorrected to *stalking*, which might be a red flag). Publishers frown on plagiarism because they're dramatic.

Anyway, I just wanted to put that little caveat here because this isn't a self-help book; it's a self-reflective book that will prayerfully lead to God-help.

Let's start with something light (you know, the way politics at Thanksgiving dinner is light or the way chocolate cheesecake is light):

In childhood, who did you have to be in order to be loved?

I'm going to put a handy chart here so you can see which one of these you most identify with, and then we'll break it down a bit.

CHILDHOOD ROLE	CHILD TRAITS	ADULT PATTERNS
The Hero (the Responsible One)	High-achieving, perfectionistic, obedient, takes care of others	Overfunctioning, people-pleasing, struggles to rest or delegate, defines worth by productivity
The Mascot (the Entertainer)	Funny, distracts from tension, avoids conflict using humor	Uses humor or lightheartedness to deflect pain, avoids emotional depth, struggles with vulnerability
The Invisible One (the Lost Child)	Quiet, withdrawn, stays out of the way, avoids conflict	Emotionally disconnected, low self-advocacy, has a hard time identifying needs, may feel invisible

CHILDHOOD ROLE	CHILD TRAITS	ADULT PATTERNS
The Scapegoat (the Rebel)	Acts out, distracts from family pain, labeled "the problem"	Self-sabotaging behaviors, chronic guilt or shame, mistrusts authority, may resist healthy intimacy
The Caretaker (the Pleaser)	Emotionally attuned to others, takes care of caregivers, suppresses own needs	Codependent tendencies, has a hard time setting boundaries, defines identity through others' well-being

Well, look at that—you found one, didn't you? You can thank Virginia Satir for that.[3]

These roles don't develop in a vacuum—they're survival strategies that children develop in response to their family environment. When a family system is under stress (addiction, mental illness, financial pressure, marital conflict, or even just the normal challenges of life), children unconsciously take on roles that help maintain stability and ensure they stay connected to their caregivers.

The Hero child learns that being perfect and responsible brings praise and reduces family stress. They become little adults, often parenting their own parents, because they discover that achievement and helpfulness make them valuable. The Mascot realizes that making people laugh diffuses tension and helps them avoid painful realities. The Invisible One figures out that being invisible and undemanding prevents them from adding to the family's burdens. The Scapegoat acts out, often unconsciously, to distract everyone from deeper problems—their "bad" behavior gives the family something to focus on other than the real issues. The Caretaker becomes hypervigilant to others' emotions, learning to manage everyone's feelings to keep the peace.

These roles serve a crucial purpose in childhood—they help children feel safe and connected in environments that feel unpredictable or overwhelming. The problem is that what works for a seven-year-old trying to navigate family dysfunction doesn't work for a thirty-seven-year-old trying to build healthy relationships.

As adults, we keep playing these roles even when they no longer serve us because they're deeply ingrained. They feel like our identity rather than just a strategy we learned.

The Hero fears: "If I'm not perfect, I'm worthless."

The Mascot fears: "If I'm not entertaining, I'll be abandoned."

The Invisible One fears: "If I speak up, I'll be rejected."

The Scapegoat fears: "I'm fundamentally bad and unlovable."

The Caretaker fears: "If I don't take care of everyone, I'll be alone."

The beautiful and difficult truth is that these roles are evidence of your strength and adaptability as a child, not your brokenness. You figured out how to survive and stay loved in challenging circumstances.

But now? It's exhausting. Never ending. Painful.

Now it's time to let your authentic self emerge.

Taking Off the Mask

At any moment, we could be calling the curtain down because we've been caught. That's because having to *be* something is different from *being* something. You might have felt like you had to be the straight-A student, but your identity isn't "achiever." Maybe you felt like you had to mediate family relationships, but your identity isn't "peacekeeper." You feel like an impostor because you haven't quite come to understand that yet. I think people are really feeling this disconnect these days, because there was a 75 percent increase in online searches for the term *impostor syndrome* in 2024.

So where is the line? How do we know when we've slipped into the act?

Pay attention to whether you are presenting yourself or being present.

Depending on which category you fit into, there are patterns you will start to pick up on when you slip back into roles that may not serve you well anymore.

Say you're the rebel. I like to pretend on that one, because I am a firstborn so I didn't have this luxury. My sister, however, went through a goth phase that involved a boyfriend who smelled like patchouli and had a very confusing nose-to-ear chain situation going on. He turned out to be delightful but did have a love for *The Rocky Horror Picture Show* that I could not reconcile.

So in the event that you're the rebel, start to notice when you feel like you're doing things just to be contrary or to push back on authority. Acknowledge what you're doing and ask yourself why. Maybe you're pushing back because you felt like everyone always talked over you and you had to be aggressive to be heard. It might be that you felt like you were only noticed when you were acting out.

When you catch yourself performing, ask, "What am I afraid will happen if I don't?"

This gets to the deeper fear quickly. If you're being extra funny, maybe you're afraid people will be bored by the real you. If you're overachieving, maybe you're afraid of being seen as lazy or worthless.

Practice one "authentic moment" per day.

It could be admitting you don't know something, sharing a real struggle instead of saying "I'm fine," or letting someone see you without makeup. Start small and build your tolerance for being seen as imperfect.

These authentic moments don't have to be dramatic confessions or major vulnerability dumps. They're small acts of honesty that gradually expand your comfort with being seen as human rather than perfect. Maybe it's admitting to a coworker that you're nervous about a presentation instead of acting confident. Maybe it's telling your spouse you're feeling overwhelmed instead of pretending you have everything under control. Maybe it's posting a photo on social media where you look like a real person having a real day instead of a carefully curated lifestyle brand.

The goal is to practice showing up as yourself in low-risk situations so that when higher-stakes moments come, authenticity feels more natural than performance. Each time you choose honesty over image management and nothing terrible happens, you're rewiring your brain to believe that you're lovable as you are.

Start by paying attention to when you feel the urge to edit yourself or present a more polished version of reality. Notice the impulse to say, "I'm great!" when you're actually struggling. Catch yourself before you pretend to understand something you don't or before you downplay an accomplishment because you're afraid of seeming boastful.

The beautiful thing about authentic moments is that they often create connection rather than rejection. When you admit you're nervous, other people often admit they're nervous too. When you show your imperfections, others feel permission to show theirs. Authenticity is contagious in the best possible way—it gives everyone permission to be human together instead of performing separately.

Notice when you feel exhausted after social interactions.

That's often a sign you've been performing instead of being present. Real connection energizes you; pretending drains you. Of course, there's some room for discernment here since introverts and extroverts experience social interactions differently. But in general, there's a sense of soul-level fatigue that comes on the heels of prolonged pretending.

Stop apologizing for being human.

When you make an honest mistake, instead of saying, "I'm so sorry, I'm such an idiot," try "Oops, let me fix that." You don't have to apologize for not being perfect.

By the way, there's nothing wrong with the traits we discussed earlier. It's not bad to have opinions or to be funny. It's amazing to be a peacekeeper or a talented athlete; in and of themselves, they are just aspects of who God made you to be. Those things are important, but they aren't the reasons you are loved.

We feel like impostors because we know the bullet is fake and we don't want the jig to be up.

Here's a radical thought: Maybe the jig is supposed to be up before it kills us; maybe we aren't unscathed at the end, but we live out the truest version of ourselves. Maybe walking with a limp is better than running away.

Who Are You . . . Really?

And now it's time to head to the deep, where we've got a fella who's wildly qualified to speak into this topic. Oh, Jacob. You and your mom must have been the originators of the term *enmeshed.* Sweet Jakey boy lived much of his life in a performance that was driven by some odd family dynamics and the desire to meet expectations.

Jacob's Story

For more about the story of Jacob and his journey from pretender to beloved of God, see Genesis 25–35.

Identity was the central theme of Jacob's life. He had an illustrious bio that included giving soup to his brother in exchange for his brother's birthright and accidentally marrying the ugly sister of the girl he actually wanted to marry (it was a setup, and apparently he didn't realize it until the next day, so I think it's safe to say it was a rager of a party). Have no fear, he did eventually marry the pretty one as well.

Before the wifey adventure, Jacob's mom convinced him to glue goat hair on his arms so his ailing and blind dad would think he was his hairy twin brother. Why? Because she wanted herrrr precioussss to receive the blessing Esau was supposed to get. I mean, she literally made him pretend to be someone else—talk about impostor syndrome. I feel the need to mention something here that is never illustrated in children's Bibles, and it's a fact I just recently learned. Y'all. Jacob was SEVENTY-SEVEN ACTUAL YEARS OLD AT THIS POINT. This really puts a whole new spin on things. Not only was he obeying his mother, he was doing so as a geriatric man. Ew.

God bless the man (don't worry, He will), his name actually means "swindler." In fact, the twins struggled in the womb, and Jacob grabbed hold of his brother's ankle as they were coming into the world. Did I mention his name also means "heel grabber?" What do we in the psychology biz like to call him? Job security.

I'm really grateful God included folks like Jacob in Scripture. At face value, he was a kid who came into the world with some uphill battles and a family that had, at best, some trust and codependency issues. Thousands of years separate us, but we all come into this life the same way he did. Into broken homes and self-doubt and sibling rivalries.

The folks we read about in the Bible lived three-dimensional lives that expand far beyond the pages. They had petty arguments and played favorites and lied and struggled with commitment.

Anyway, after tricking dad and ripping off his brother, Jacob ran for his life. He worked for his uncle, married his cousins, and ended up with lots of kids and plenty of servants and animals. Years later he ditched his uncle and headed into the wilderness with his large and complicated family. After a little traveling, he found out that Esau was hot on his trail, and all signs pointed to a rocky reunion. It looked like his past had found him, and given the fact that his brother had four hundred men with him, it wasn't looking great for Jacob and crew. So he sent his two wives and eleven children ahead and hung out alone for a little bit.

It seemed that everything had caught up with him. Years of scheming and lying and manipulating had come to a head, and the miles were closing between him and his day of reckoning. He couldn't keep up the act anymore.

Sometimes God allows us to reach the end of our ability to maintain the facade. The very thing we've been running from—being found out, being seen as we really are—becomes the doorway to freedom. Jacob's moment of reckoning wasn't his punishment; it was his invitation to stop performing and start receiving.

Wrestling the Right Opponent

There was a slight interruption to Jacob's quiet time when a wrestling match broke out between him and a stranger. Haaaatteeee it when that happens.

This didn't just happen for a minute—it went on for hours.

Somewhere in the process, the man put Jacob's hip out of its socket—but the match didn't end there. At daybreak, the stranger told Jacob to let him go, but Jacob refused and uttered a sentence that leads to one of my favorite interactions in all of Scripture: "I will not let you go unless you bless me."

Whoa, what? Bless him? Who wants to get a blessing from some random guy who attacked him and then popped his hip out of the socket? Well, I guess anyone would if they knew what Jacob did: He had been wrestling with God Himself, and he was not going to surrender until he was blessed by Him.

Let's rewind for a moment, shall we? I don't want you to miss the details here, because they tell parts of the story that give it depth and color. Context, context, context—that's of utmost importance when reading the Bible.

Since the moment he was born, Jacob had been a trickster. No, seriously—from the actual moment. As I said, his name means "swindler." I'm not saying we are defined by our given names, but in this case, Jacob certainly lived up to the, umm, baby shower theme? He'd done his fair share of swindling during his life and left a wake of repercussions based on bad decisions, and now they'd finally caught up to him. I've been there, that's for sure.

What's beautiful about this wrestling match is that it represents the difference between wrestling with God and wrestling with the world. Jacob had spent his entire life wrestling with people—manipulating circumstances, trying to control outcomes, fighting for position and blessing through his own schemes. But that night, he was finally wrestling with the right opponent.

When we're living from our false self, we're constantly wrestling with the world—trying to prove our worth, manage other people's opinions, control how we're perceived. We exhaust ourselves fighting battles that can never give us what we're truly looking for. You can't manipulate your way into authentic love. You can't perform your way into genuine acceptance. You can't scheme your way into true belonging.

But wrestling with God is different. It's not about trying to get something from Him through trickery or performance—it's about refusing to let go until He shows you who you really are. It's about holding on through the pain and darkness until He speaks your true name over you. It's about being willing to be wounded in the process because you know that His blessing is worth more than your ability to walk away unscathed.

Jacob's limp became proof of his authentic encounter with God. It was evidence that he'd stopped running from the truth and started running toward it. The swindler who had always tried to get blessings through deception finally received a genuine blessing through honest desperation. His weakness became the mark of his transformation—not something to hide, but something to carry with honor.

This is what authentic spiritual transformation looks like. Not the clean, pretty version we hear about in testimonies, but the messy, painful, beautiful process of being seen fully by God and discovering that His love doesn't require us to be anyone other than who we actually are.

Basically, Jacob had nothing to lose.

Including the wrestling match. Even though he was wounded, he was also determined. Besides, what's the worst that could happen at that point? Then God asked him a question that could have sounded a little depressing: "What's your name?"

I mean, of all people to forget.

I'm guessing you've figured out that God didn't really wonder what Jacob's name was—He wasn't making polite conversation. He wanted Jacob to come as face-to-face with himself as he was to God. No more running. No more hiding. *You and I both know who you are, but I know something you don't: It won't always be this way.*

Jacob answered with one word: his name. And with that, God told him he would no longer be called Jacob but instead would be called Israel. He told him that he would take this name because he had fought with God and man and had won. With that, Jacob walked away with a limp—a reminder of both his confession and his redemption.

But wait! Did my editors fail to correct what I just wrote? Nope. I said *Jacob* walked away, not Israel. Turns out, God hadn't changed his name yet despite the version of the story you may be familiar with.

When Esau saw Jacob on the horizon, he ran and embraced him. Esau showed no signs of animosity, and he even thanked Jacob for sending some animals and other gifts to him in anticipation of their reunion. Even though Jacob told Esau he would be following behind him with his family so they could settle in the same town, he actually took a different route and set up the home front in a place called Succoth. I don't blame him—it's hard to resist the allure of a place with a name like that. An all-inclusive seaside town with sweeping views and the world-famous Succoth Spa.

Please take note of the fact that while Jacob reconciled with his brother, he did not follow him. Sometimes we have to take stock of who we are healthier without—can I get an *amen* on that?

Eventually God told Jacob it was time to head back toward Canaan, which was probably a relief to the wives, because no one wants their kids to go to Succoth High.

Before he hit the road, Jacob told his wives there was one little thing they needed to take care of: get rid of all the idols they'd been carrying. They did as they were asked, and Jacob buried the idols deep in the ground before heading out. We don't know exactly what those idols were, but it's likely they were small charms that people believed brought them good luck or prosperity.

They may have had value, but they were worth absolutely nothing. They had no power. They were false shields, and they were heavy.

Masks can be idols. They're valuable because you think they have protected you, but they actually have no power and they're heavy.

Lay them down, friend.

God knows the truest part of you, and He loves you.

That's one of those sentences you might read quickly and skim past, but I want you to sit with it for just a moment and allow it to sink deep into your bones. He looks past the false selves you've created because He knows that underneath all of them is the fear that really matters: *Would they love me if they knew?*

And the One who really matters says He does.

You Are Loved: No Mask Required

I told you that Jacob walked away with a limp, but I haven't yet told you the rest of the story. Several chapters and events take place, culminating in the decision to lay down every idol and move forward in faith.

And it is at that moment God spoke: "Your name is Jacob, but you will no longer be called Jacob; your name will be Israel."

Israel. The name that means "one who struggles with God."

God wasn't ignoring the fact that Jacob had a less-than-stellar past and reputation, but He wasn't leaving it there either.

Jacob had had enough of running, and he admitted that he couldn't do it anymore. Have you?

You aren't the achiever, the scapegoat, or the rebel. You are the beloved of God.

Not that it's always easy to remember that—I get it. It's almost like you have to practice believing it and test it out for a bit; it's not an overnight process.

People will remember you as you have been, and some of them would prefer you stay that way because it suits them. Trust me, when you go home at Christmas, you'll slip back into the role you've had there.

I bet Jacob had to have a lot of awkward conversations with people in the coming days. He had to gather up his family and have the old "God changed my name, so now you have to call me something else" conversation. Then he had to do the same whenever he saw people out and about.

"Jacob! How the heck are you?"

"So, funny story, Mike . . ."

Not to mention the paperwork. The Succoth DMV is notoriously understaffed.

You can change your name to make people love you, or you can love the One who will change it for you. You can wrestle with the world over the name they've given you or wrestle with God to remind you who you really are.

What is the limp you're still trying to hide—the proof of your wrestling—that might actually be the most honest part of your story?

Here's the beautiful part of being your true self: Those who genuinely know you don't judge you for having a limp because they know how you got it. They know your imperfections point to a perfect God.

Maybe it's time you stop apologizing for the limp that makes you look imperfect and start living like someone who fought too hard to call it anything less than a miracle.

A Benediction for Pretenders

May you learn to take off the masks that hide who you really are and remember that God formed you—exactly you.

May you stop wrestling and remember that you already have a name.

May you stop striving to be someone you aren't for people who will never truly know you.

When you're tempted to believe you have to be someone else to be loved, hear the voice of the Lord telling you it isn't so.

As you walk through your day, I pray you come face-to-face with reminders of your value, both on earth and in heaven.

2

You Won't Miss a Thing

You are accepted.

Sometimes we need to let go of the ones who make us feel left out to find the ones who make us feel at home.

UNKNOWN

I'm not sure if I will even be able to get through this story without crying, but it's one of those that will always hurt. It's the worst kind of hurt, because it's the kind that comes along with being a mom and feeling helpless.

One of my daughters had just started college, and I was having a really hard time adjusting to the fact that I wasn't seeing her and didn't know much about what her days looked like. She was about to go to her first formal dance, and she sent me pictures of the dresses she had found and told me about her ideas for hair and makeup. I was so excited for her to have this first experience at school. The day of the dance came, and she checked in with friends to see if they were all getting together to get ready, but they said they were just going to meet up later.

She got ready by herself in her little dorm room, and I can't help but imagine her nerves while she thought about what it would be like and who would be there. She did her hair and makeup and slipped into her dress before happening upon a series of photos showing her friends getting ready together.

I can't tell you why it happened and she got over it pretty quickly, but I can't say the same for myself (as evidenced by the fact that I am still teary-eyed now). I felt far away and unable to shield her from the inevitability of feeling left out. She took selfies to show me, but she wasn't in their pictures. She went on to have a great night and is still close with many of those girls . . . what I'm saying is that it wasn't something that went on forever.

But that's not how it feels in the moment. It triggers all the awful thoughts you already have about yourself, and guess what? It's everywhere. Gone are the days when people could leave you out without you knowing. We are living in the time of group texts, social media posts, and location trackers.

The cruelty of modern FOMO is that it's inescapable in ways our parents never had to navigate. Your grandmother might have found out she was excluded from the church ladies' luncheon when someone mentioned it weeks later in passing. You find out in real time, with full-color documentation and GPS coordinates.

Social media has turned every gathering into a broadcast, every inside joke into public evidence of your exclusion. You're not just missing the event—you're watching it unfold in high definition through Instagram stories and Snapchat updates.

You see them getting ready together, arriving together, laughing together, all while you're sitting at home wondering why your phone has been so quiet.

The technology designed to connect us has become a magnifying glass for our insecurities, amplifying every moment of exclusion until it feels like evidence of our fundamental unworthiness.

Just the other day one of my younger daughter Charlotte's friends came over in tears because she was told a sleepover had been canceled, but she had the location of all the girls invited and she was the only one in a different place on the map.

There are a million and one ways we can feel like we are on the outside looking in, and it's heartbreaking to feel like you aren't wanted.

But what if you aren't being left out—what if you're being positioned exactly where God wants you?

The Real Pain of Being Left Out

Although it's a term we hear thrown around a lot these days, FOMO is a more serious issue than we realize and has a lot of layers that are worth dissecting. It's a lot more than "They all went to dinner and didn't invite me." Let's sort through some of the underlying issues together.

You should know that brain studies reveal that feelings of FOMO actually trigger the same parts of your brain as physical pain, and the loop it takes when you feel left out is anything but helpful. When you feel left out, you're more likely to scroll to find what researchers call "social surrogacy," which leads to depression and anxiety because it emphasizes your loneliness.[1] It hurts, and for logical reasons.

Your brain is essentially treating your social rejection like it's a physical wound. You might notice that you feel your chest getting tight or your breathing changing—your nervous system doesn't distinguish between being chased by a bear and being left out of brunch plans.

Is It Bears or Brunch? would actually be a killer book title.

When we dig deeper into what's really happening when FOMO hits, we discover it's not really about missing events—it's about questioning our worth.

Am I worth wanting around? Ouch. That hurts just to write. When we feel left out, we immediately wonder if we're the kind of person who adds value when included. We want to think we would be missed if we weren't there, but secretly we think they might not notice—or, worse, enjoy it more.

This worthiness question reveals something deeper than social insecurity—it exposes our fundamental uncertainty about whether we matter. FOMO isn't really about fear of missing out on fun; it's about fear of confirmation that we're not essential, not valued, not chosen. Every exclusion feels like evidence in a case we're already building against ourselves.

We have to remember that there's a difference between being valued and being chosen for specific moments. You can be deeply valued by someone who still doesn't include you in every gathering. You can be essential to someone's life without being essential to their Tuesday night dinner plans. Worth isn't measured by invitations received; it's an inherent quality that exists regardless of who recognizes it at any given moment.

The tragedy is that when we let FOMO convince us we're not worth wanting around, we start showing up differently in the relationships we do have. We become performative, trying to prove our value instead of simply being ourselves. We start measuring every interaction for signs of rejection, which makes us exhausting to be around. The very fear that drives us to seek inclusion often creates the exact behaviors that make inclusion less likely.

I hate to admit that my mind doesn't automatically jump to assuming the best; I instantly imagine a slight was done deliberately. They're probably all sitting around talking about how much they can't stand me and how much better it is without me. More than likely, it's an oversight or it was just how the circumstances played out.

Here's the truth, though: There are times when it *is* deliberate. My daughter's friend was intentionally left out of a sleepover, and there was no confusion over that fact. When she was at our house, she kept tearing up a little and then making a comment about how it was silly to be upset. I told her that not only was it not silly, it was appropriate. It's okay to grieve hard moments—it doesn't make you a shallow person. I don't think the reasonable response is ever to just buck up and shut off your emotions. I think it's becoming comfortable bringing them to Jesus.

I understand that different groups of people hang out, and I tell my kids constantly that they aren't going to be invited to everything, because that's a part of life. Don't cry foul just because a couple of your buddies got ice cream without you. I will also say that if you sense a pattern of meanness in a group or if you feel like you're being pushed out, those are not your people. Don't fight for inclusion.

We are grown-ups here; if someone is going to act like a mean girl in her clique, I will let her look absurd, but I'm not taking the bait. If you think about the people you love and respect and truly enjoy spending time with, you'll note that they aren't the ones who act like queen bees. Instead of choosing their hive, they love well and hold a special place for people.

Do you know how many times I have cried about being left out of something I never even wanted to be a part of? I wasn't going to go to the party, but I really would have loved an invite. Sometimes the event is with people I don't even love being around, but the sheer fact that I didn't make the cut feels brutal.

We're so afraid to miss out on things that we even commit to going places we don't want to go just so we can say we were a part of it. We were made for relationship and a sense of belonging, so it's natural to seek community. But if we're looking to a group of people to define our worth, we will live a lonely existence.

Alone Is Not the Same as Lonely

Here's something FOMO gets wrong: It confuses being alone with being lonely, and it mistakes solitude for rejection.

There's a profound difference between chosen solitude and imposed isolation, but FOMO makes us afraid of both.

When we're so terrified of missing out, we lose the ability to be content in our own company or to recognize when God might be calling us into a season of quiet. We interpret every moment of aloneness as evidence that we're unwanted, rather than considering that solitude might be exactly what our souls need.

Some of the most significant spiritual growth happens not in the noise of constant social engagement but in the stillness of being alone with God. When we're always chasing the next invitation, the next gathering, the next proof that we belong somewhere, we miss the invitation to belong fully to ourselves and to Him.

Jesus Himself regularly withdrew from crowds, even from His closest friends, to spend time alone with the Father. If we applied our FOMO logic to His life, we'd say He was missing out on ministry opportunities, on relationship-building moments, on chances to be included in whatever His disciples were doing. But His solitude wasn't isolation—it was intentional positioning for the work God had called Him to do.

Sometimes what we interpret as social rejection is actually divine redirection. The plans that fall through, the invitations that don't come, the moments when we're left with just ourselves and God—these aren't punishments or evidence of our unworthiness. They're opportunities to discover that we're never actually alone, even when we're by ourselves.

It's easy to say we are settled in the fact that our worth comes from Jesus, but it's not at all easy to feel that in moments of rejection. It sort of feels like when you're the only one not invited to the movies, so your dad tells you he wants to hang out. It's sweet, but kind of in a sad way.

I want to matter enough to be included. I don't want to hear about it—I want to be a part of it. When I'm not, I never start by being angry at the people who left me out. I immediately wonder what's wrong with me.

It's good to be reminded that not everyone around me is the same way, because the freedom to not see myself as the problem feels very intriguing. A few years ago, my daughter Kate went to a party with a boy she was dating, but she didn't know anyone else there. She is very social and comfortable in her own skin, so she doesn't really feel like she has to prove herself. She came home early without her boyfriend, and I asked her what happened. She said she told him she was going to take off but that he should just stay and have fun. When I asked her why, she said, "Well, I was hanging out with a group of people, and I was making some really good jokes. They didn't laugh at all, and I just realized they weren't my people, so I took off."

What? We can do that?

She wasn't unkind about it—she just hugged everyone and made her way out because it wasn't her thing. I can't tell you how hard I laughed when she told me that, because honest to goodness, I love the moments when it seems like your dysfunction somehow dodged genetics.

She is not the slightest bit cocky, but she's settled in who she is. She just kind of assumes everyone's life gets better when she's in the room, and in fairness, she's not wrong. She isn't a gossip. She isn't a liar. She is the first to root for the underdog and take people under her wing. She uses "Ma'am" and "Sir" like they're going out of style, and she is one of the very few people on planet earth I genuinely find shockingly funny. She assumes you love her until you tell her differently—the polar opposite of her mother. There is an ease about people who don't see others as competition, and it's refreshing.

Here's the point: Kate has always been popular, but she's never tried to be for a day in her life. If she isn't included, she doesn't assume she was excluded.

In other words, she doesn't look to the world to understand her worth.

What a wild existence it must be.

Don't misunderstand what I'm saying: Our worth comes only from Jesus and because of Jesus, but it can still hurt when we're left out. Both can be true.

What to Do When FOMO Hits

For times when feelings of rejection start to bubble up in you, let's talk through a few practical ways to work through them with the help of the Holy Spirit.

Focus on the relationships that are choosing you.

Look around at the people who are actually in your life—not just in a "be grateful" way that dismisses disappointment, but in an internal way that makes you ask yourself who you might be overlooking while focusing on someone who isn't there.

Remember that being excluded might be a form of redirection.

Even though that might seem like a way to make yourself feel better, the reality is that this is often how God works. What you think is being passed over is actually positioning, because He has something better. Look around you—where could God be working? What might He have right in front of you that He wants you to see?

Assume positive intent until proven otherwise.

When you don't get invited, try assuming it wasn't personal before jumping to "They must not like me." Maybe they thought you were busy, maybe it was a small group, maybe they genuinely forgot. Start with curiosity instead of immediately wondering what's wrong with you.

Notice when you're fishing for inclusion versus actually wanting to go.

When you catch yourself upset about missing something, ask, *Did I really want to be there, or do I just want to feel wanted?* Sometimes the hurt is about the invitation itself, not the event.

Stop performing for people who make you work for their approval.

If you're constantly trying to prove your worth to a group that consistently overlooks you, that's not your crowd. Find the people who are excited you showed up, not the ones you have to win over.

Bring your hurt to God instead of hiding it.

When FOMO hits, be honest with God about feeling left out instead of trying to spiritual-bypass your way to contentment. He can handle your disappointment and your questions about why it happened.

You're worthy even if you feel like the party is about someone else, and you're worthy when you think you missed the best part. If you don't believe me, stay tuned.

Missing Out on Favor

There are several FOMO moments in the Bible, but let's kick it off with one that happens in a parable Jesus taught. It goes like this.

The Older Brother's Story

For more about the story of the older brother and his FOMO, see Luke 15:11-32.

A man had two sons. The younger one went to his dad and told him he would like his inheritance early. "I know you're alive, but I'd like to enjoy that now, thank you." His dad gave it to him and the kid split. He was headed to big city life and wasn't going to look back.

Things did not go well. He wasted his money and a famine set in, so he headed back home. Before he could even reach the house, his father took off in a sprint and welcomed him back with open arms. Patriarchs did not run back then, because it was considered shameful and embarrassing, yet he couldn't help himself.

The runaway was well aware of the fact that he had done wrong and had no business showing up there, but his words were hidden in the folds of his father's cloak. Instead of sending the boy away, he clung to him. He gave him a ring, a robe, and a party.

Meanwhile, the wild child's brother had been out working because, firstborn. When he came home, he saw that there was some kind of celebration, so he asked one of the workers what was going on.

"Deadbeat's back! Check out the robe your dad put on him. Yeah, he got a ring and a personalized cookie cake too. What a day."

Dad came out to beg his son to join them, but it would not be an easy sell. This guy had been to enough therapy to know how to speak his truth, so he let loose.

"Why are you rewarding him? He's been out spending money on prostitutes, and you never even gave me a young goat!"

This feels anticlimactic, but I am not personally familiar with the simple days when the best way to celebrate a kid running a marathon was to have a nice little goat for him at the finish line.

Brother was not done. He brought up the prostitutes and the goats again, because these seem to be his strongest bullet points.

Pops dropped a bomb.

"My son, you are always with me. Everything I have is yours. But we had to celebrate and be glad, because this brother of yours was dead and is alive again."

Dang.

Way to put a damper on the goat argument—you know he'd had that sucker in his back pocket for years.

It wasn't really about the party; it was about the fact that he felt like he was the good one and now he was missing out on his dad's favor.

Maybe you know the feeling: Someone else is getting what's best instead of you, and even worse, they don't deserve it.

He Won't Let You Miss a Thing

I have to say, though, if there's an award for the worst FOMO moment in the history of time, it would surely go to Thomas.

I know I shouldn't have favorites, but the good Lord knows how I love the disciple Thomas. He just kind of fumbles through his faith, but even when he gets it wrong, it's coming from a good place. He's famously known as "the doubter," but that title really doesn't do him justice; he was loyal to the Lord and made some of the boldest claims of love in the New Testament.

Thomas's Story

For more about the story of Thomas and his fear of missing out, see John 20:24-29; Luke 24:41-43.

Let me set the scene: Jesus was dead. He'd been buried. The dream was over—He must not have been all the things His friends thought He was.

The disciples had gathered together in an upper room (without Thomas, apparently) and seemed to be having a pretty normal evening (as normal as it can be when you're trying to avoid being murdered) when a guest showed up unannounced. It was none other than the resurrected Jesus.

He reassured them and then asked a couple of odd questions: "Why are you troubled? Why did doubts rise in your minds?"

I feel certain that crucifixion would feel pretty final. And troubling. And would probably cause doubt.

He showed them His hands and feet and assured them that He was alive and well. They were in shock and still struggling to believe it was Him.

Don't worry—Jesus had a plan.

"Do you have anything here to eat?"

It feels fair that He would be hungry after His last few days. Luckily for Him, it's broiled fish night in the upper room, and He ate in front of them. You may be wondering why the King of the world couldn't figure out how to feel full without eating, but that's not the point of this moment. He was showing them that He wasn't a figment of their imagination—a ghost can't eat food.

Eventually He left, and at some point, Thomas showed up. We don't know where he'd been, but it's safe to say he was about to experience the rainbow of FOMO colors.

We aren't privy to the conversation, but we can only imagine the way he reacted when he found out he missed the ultimate dinner guest.

"Yeah, He was here, Thomas. We all saw Him and spent time with Him—man, was He hungry. Check out the selfie—He looks good given the situation, doesn't He?"

Thomas stared at them in shock.

"No, seriously, Thomas. It was Him. He showed us His hands and feet. He's back."

Thomas was less than pleased and made a bold declaration: "I won't believe it until I see it for myself. Until I touch His wounds and see what you have seen."

Just a couple of things I want to point out here: Jesus knew Thomas wasn't going to be there. He didn't walk in and roll His eyes because He thought they would all be together.

He left Thomas out deliberately because He knew that ultimately this would lead to trust.

"Why did You let me miss it, Lord?"

Because I had something better.

Seven days passed, and Jesus returned. These weren't wasted days; they were set aside and holy. They were days of doubt that would lead to true belief.

I love that Jesus didn't condemn him for doubting, and in fact, He invited him to do the exact three things Thomas said he would have to do before he believed. Think about it—Jesus knew what Thomas needed even though He wasn't in the room to hear the words.

Here's one of the best parts of the story—and one that is often missed: Thomas thought he knew what he needed in order to believe, but his human beliefs seemed to disappear in the wake of seeing Christ again. The text never tells us that Thomas did any of the things he said were mandatory for him to believe. In fact, the first thing he did was declare that Jesus was his Lord and his God.

Once again, Thomas came through with a one-liner for the ages.

This was the first time Scripture records anyone calling Jesus by this name, which is significant. He is human and deity, the true Son of God.

I hope you've figured this out by now: Nothing in Scripture is an accident.

The one who thought he'd been left out made the first true declaration of the identity of God. He knew his worth because he knew Jesus' worth.

Our fear of missing out on things hinges on a false principle: that we are missing out on the best thing.

In fact, sometimes it turns out to be a good thing that we weren't there—rumor has it that everyone at the sleepover got sick because the young goat soufflé was undercooked.

A Benediction for Those with FOMO

May the Lord remind you that wherever you are today is exactly where you're meant to be.

Even when it seems you are missing out, may you remember that you are never left out of His presence.

When exclusion stings, may you see it not as rejection, but as an invitation to lean into the Father, who delights in you.

Sometimes God holds us back not to punish us but to protect us—or to draw us into a deeper intimacy with Him than we would have found elsewhere.

You have not been forgotten, beloved. You have been remembered by the One who loves you more than you will ever understand.

Your worth is determined not by the world's attention or indifference but by the unshakable truth that you are chosen in every moment of every day.

May you rest in that today and always.

Amen.

3

More Than a Guest in Someone Else's Story

You are chosen.

The tip of the neighbour's iceberg often looks very nice.

ROY A. NGANSOP

One day while looking in the kitchen cabinets for a bowl, it occurred to me that owning fifty-six cookbooks is excessive for a woman who doesn't, for lack of a better word, *cook.*

And yet I'm always on the hunt for more. There's something satisfying about studying the pages of beautiful food and lining up the books so I'm an arm's length from instruction on everything from hosting a perfect Christmas dinner to understanding the difference between slicing and dicing. There are three channels I will watch for hours on end, and two of them are food related.

Again, all of this is intriguing mostly because I don't like cooking, and cooking has made it clear that the feeling is mutual.

With all this said, I go through spurts where I decide I am one gadget away from hosting a food show. I reason that if I had the knife that cuts pennies, I could wow my guests with my homemade Bolognese.

So I choose a few recipes and head to the grocery store, where I stroll along the spice aisle like I'm the queen of cumin, artfully reach for the flat-leaf parsley instead of the curly kind, and make casual conversation with the person behind me in line while I lift my exotic bounty onto the belt.

I will also confess that once it's time to cook, I tend to wait until no one is around. That's not because I don't want their help—it's because I like to pretend I'm preparing it for a camera. For what it's worth, I've probably imaginary-produced at least one hundred episodes that all end with me dipping a wooden spoon into some kind of concoction and closing my eyes to convince the audience my Sicilian grandmother would give me a standing ovation.

I learned pretty early on that what makes the shows feel like magic has to do with pre-measuring, having salt in an open container so you can pinch it with your pretty nails, the nonexistence of prep work and cleanup, the marked absence of screaming children, and being on a first-name basis with the butcher. Incidentally, you will use the same pretty nails to effortlessly slide through the tape, unwrap the thick paper around the steak, and reach for a pair of tongs, all while never looking away from the camera.

Because it's easy. Look how easy it is.

I don't care how many times my husband, Todd, tells me he didn't eat the last piece of salad because he found my blood on it (this is a true story, and while the menu item varies, my actual blood has made a guest appearance at dinner more times than the Barefoot Contessa's husband, Jeffrey), it's only a matter of time before I start the cycle again. And it's never less exciting, regardless of the fact that the teenager in the deli department refuses to make eye contact while I ask him questions about his summer in Nantucket. I don't know how else we're going to get this relational ball rolling, Brandon.

And do I measure out the ingredients in little glass dishes? I sure do. Do I have at least two cutting boards, a sizzling pan, a pot of boiled water, and a few gripping stories about how the dish is tied to my childhood in India/Malaysia/Greece/Italy/Mexico/a seaside beach town in New England? Of course. The smells will bring me back, but not enough to derail me from the joy of the present moment. It's just so much fun to cook. Fun and easy. Easy and fun. And all the avocados are ripe in Cooktown today, as you would imagine.

Two things inevitably happen during the cooking process: I burn myself and I swear. Sometimes those are related, and sometimes they aren't. There are moments when I think to myself, *Wow! I'm enjoying this.* The other 95 percent of the time I'm angry at everything and everyone and start plotting ways to find the bubbly chef who wrote the recipe and ask her how it is that she has managed to find the holy land between eating pancetta every day and wearing jeans she bought in the toddler department.

One night I was cleaning up after another failed meal, and as I put the saffron away, it occurred to me that I had absolutely no idea what saffron was. I googled it, because what else do you do?

Five minutes later, I could tell you the plant it comes from, what weather conditions are most favorable for growth, its country of origin, and that saffron's taste profile includes words like *haylike*, which is neither helpful nor persuasive as a description of something I'm planning to eat.

The thing is, I'm not really trying to become a chef—I'm trying to perform in someone else's show instead of living my own story.

Here's what's really happening with my cookbook obsession: I'm not just buying recipes; I'm buying into a fantasy version of myself. This fantasy version of myself has time to make homemade pasta and never orders pizza. She's domestic without being boring, creative without being chaotic, and somehow manages to look like she just stepped out of a magazine in the midst of it.

I am confronted with about one hundred different potential versions of myself: the one who vacations, the one who volunteers, the one who loves high fashion, the one who effortlessly plans her children's day.

It's hard to live your own life when you're trying too hard to live someone else's.

Keeping Up with the Joneses: International Edition

When we think about comparison in childhood, we immediately recall hearing things like, "Your brother didn't have any trouble with his driving test," or "You're the best singer at the school." We've been trained to scan the world to see how we stack up next to other people, and it's no surprise that it's harder today than it has been in the past, based on the overwhelming access we have to other people's lives.

Women didn't start comparing themselves to other women in the 1950s, friends—it has always been this way. It's human nature to gauge ourselves and our lives based on others' lives. Who has the most successful business? The coziest home? The best bread recipe? The world has changed, but much has stayed the same. Anxiety existed. Depression existed.

What didn't exist? Forty percent off goat hair at Hobby Lobby just in time for the TikTok challenge. Look how far we've come.

Social media has weaponized comparison in ways previous generations couldn't have imagined. Our grandmothers might have compared themselves to their neighbors or the women at church, but they weren't bombarded with carefully curated images from thousands of strangers every day. They didn't have to see the vacation photos, the perfect kitchens, the romantic date nights, and the milestone achievements of people they've never met, all presented as if this is just normal, everyday life.

Here's what makes modern comparison even more insidious: It's no longer just about keeping up with the Joneses next door. Now we're trying to keep up with the Joneses in California, the Smiths in New York, and the influencer in Nashville who somehow makes motherhood look like a photo shoot. We're comparing our real, messy, unfiltered lives to highlight reels that have been edited, filtered, and strategically posted for maximum impact.

The algorithm is designed to show us more of what we engage with, so if you linger on someone's perfect kitchen renovation, you'll be fed more perfect kitchens. If you watch someone's morning routine video, you'll get more morning routines. Before you know it, your entire feed is filled with people who seem to have mastered every area of life you feel like you're failing at. You wake up feeling decent about your life and go to bed feeling like everyone else got a manual you never received.

What's particularly cruel is that social media makes comparison feel like research. You tell yourself you're just "getting ideas" for your own home/workout routine/parenting style, but really you're studying other people's lives like you're cramming for a test on how to be a better person. You bookmark their posts, screenshot their outfits, and try to reverse-engineer their success, all while feeling increasingly inadequate about your own perfectly good life.

Here's what happens when we fall down the comparison rabbit hole: We start unconsciously trying on other people's identities like clothes. You don't just want her kitchen—you want to be the kind of person who has that kitchen. You start buying the perfume she mentions, copying her morning routine, even using her phrases in conversation without realizing it.

"Identity borrowing" is more subtle and pervasive than we realize.[1] It extends beyond the material things into personality traits and life philosophies. You're not just admiring them—you're trying to become them, piece by piece, hoping that if you can just copy enough elements of their life, you'll finally feel like you're living correctly.

The tragedy is that in trying to become someone else, we abandon the unique gifts and perspectives that make us who we are. We trade our authentic voice for an imitation of someone else's, our genuine interests for what we think we should be interested in, and our natural rhythms for routines that work for someone we don't even know.

We tell ourselves that we don't know the truth behind what we see of other people's lives, but we can't necessarily make ourselves believe it. You can tell me all day long that the couple on YouTube fights, but I have no such evidence. I'm stuck in my messy kitchen on a Tuesday morning while she's wearing a bikini in her backyard pool with the baby she pushed out of her actual body like six hours ago. Also, her husband just brought her breakfast in bed, and meanwhile I'm just wondering why people can't just run water in the oatmeal bowl before it barnacles itself on there.

Sometimes we forget that our stories are worth living—we don't have to guest-star in someone else's. I have just stumbled into a section where I will use a sentence with so much alliteration it will make your head spin: Cultivating contentment is how we combat comparison and competition.

No one cares about your seashells on the seashore anymore, lady.

Living Your Own Story

So how do we move from horizontal comparison to vertical contentment—from performing in their show to living our own story? Here are some things I've found helpful when I'm stuck in the comparison trap.

Name the real fear.

When you catch yourself studying her morning routine, scrolling through their perfect vacation photos, or researching what makes their marriage look so effortless, stop and name what's happening underneath. Don't let yourself get away with "I just want a nicer kitchen" or "I wish I could afford that vacation." Get specific about the deeper terror. Instead of saying, "I'm envious," try this: "I'm afraid God will never give me what I really want. I'm afraid He's forgotten the desires of my heart, and their life is proof that He remembers their longings but not mine." Or maybe: "I'm afraid I'm doing life wrong, and everyone else got instructions I never received."

Here's what's powerful about naming the real fear out loud: It shifts you from feeling generally bad about your life to addressing a specific fear about God's character. Instead of spiraling into "My life sucks," you're having an honest conversation with God about whether you can trust Him with your deepest longings. You're not just managing surface-level envy anymore—you're dealing with the spiritual crisis underneath.

Then go crash their vacation.

I kid. I mean, I mostly kid.

Remember that He uses everything.

I am currently sitting on what can only be described as a well-worn couch. It's a Restoration Hardware knockoff that we've had for years. The cushions are deformed because one of our enormous golden retrievers thinks he is a lap dog and likes to lie behind us on top of the couch. There is pilling that I can't seem to get rid of no matter how many gadgets I buy. I tend to notice other people's furniture because there is so much of mine that I would love to update.

I know it's a silly couch, but stick with me.

Suddenly that thing you wish was a little different in your life becomes a symbol for all the things you think are wrong with it. Every time you look at it, you get more frustrated, and eventually you start to resent it. Before you know it, you've made that poor little couch a representation of everything you want to change about your life—and the poor thing already has impostor syndrome.

Psychologists call this reframing—changing how you think about something without changing the facts. Same couch, different story. Instead of looking at the hard things in your life as evidence that something's broken, try to look for evidence that God is using them. It's one thing to say, "God, thank You that I have a place to sit," but it's even more powerful if you can remind yourself of the deeper value that is specific to you. It's more than just thanking God for provision—it's being grateful for specific providence.

I thank God for the fact that I have neighborhood children who come to sit on my well-worn couch to get advice. I'm grateful that in every nook and cranny are memories of years I can never get back. It's not generic gratitude—it's a specific acknowledgment of the things I think hold me back somehow; it's a reminder that God uses even the things I think are wrong with my life in beautiful ways.

Reframe others' wins as evidence of God's goodness.

This can be hard, but it's about training yourself to see someone else's good news without immediately measuring it against your own life. When she gets the promotion, the pregnancy, the house, the relationship, your first instinct is probably to ask, "What's wrong with me that I don't have that?" or "What did she do to deserve this that I didn't do?" Instead of letting their win become evidence against God's goodness in your life, try this: "I'm glad good things happen to people. That means good things can happen to me too." It's not about forcing fake happiness when your heart is breaking with envy. It's about breaking the habit of using their success as proof that you're failing.

Here's what I've learned: When I immediately go to "Why not me?" I'm essentially believing that there's only so much good to go around, and someone else getting some means there's less for me. But when I can genuinely think, *Good for her,* I'm reminding myself that God's goodness isn't finite. Another person's blessing doesn't diminish mine.

The goal isn't to celebrate before you can feel it—it's to stop keeping score. Their life isn't the measuring stick for yours, and their timeline isn't evidence that you're behind. Sometimes the kindest thing you can do for yourself is to get off social media, stop studying their blueprint, and focus on the story God is writing in your own life.

Challenge the belief that you're not enough.

Comparison inevitably leads us to believe there is something fundamentally wrong with us. It's more than the fact that you don't have certain things; it's that you're not the kind of person who has nice things. You don't have the job because you aren't smart enough. You don't have the relationship because you're not lovable enough. You will never look like her because you don't have the discipline.

Psychologists call this your narrative identity—the story you tell yourself about who you are and what you can expect from life.[2] When comparison becomes a habit, your narrative identity shifts into believing there's something wrong with you and that's why your life is a mess.

Here's how this works: Every time you compare yourself to someone else and come up short, you're not just feeling bad about one aspect of your life—you're editing the story of who you are. Instead of "I wish I had her kitchen," the story becomes "I'm the kind of person who can never get it together enough to have nice things." Instead of "I'd love to take a vacation like that," it becomes "I'm not the kind of person who gets to have amazing experiences."

This narrative rewriting is insidious because it starts to feel like truth instead of interpretation. You begin to believe that there are certain types of people who get certain types of lives, and you're just not one of them. You're not the career woman, you're not the organized mom, you're not the one with the happy marriage, you're not the person things work out for.

Breaking free from comparison means recognizing when you're letting other people's lives rewrite your own story and choosing to remember that God's narrative about who you are is the only one that matters.

It's hard to teach yourself to think this way because the world has ingrained comparison into every fiber of our being. But just because God sees someone else doesn't mean He doesn't see you.

No one knows this better than the team you're about to meet.

How Do You Measure Your Worth?

Today's feature film stars Jacob and his roller coaster of a love life. His leading ladies will play both sisters and wives, and it's bound to put a unique spin on holy matrimony. Also, basically everyone is related, so the beach house is full-on spring break.

Rachel and Leah's Story

For more about Rachel and Leah and their story of wrestling with comparison, see Genesis 29–30.

It starts with Jacob, who fell in love with a beautiful relative named Rachel (told you). He was so in love with her that he agreed to work for her father for seven years in order to win her hand in marriage. It passed like the blink of an eye for him because all he could dream of was the day she would be his wife.

It was finally the wedding day. Imagine his surprise when he realized Rachel's dad had pulled the old switcheroo and he was actually marrying her notably less attractive older sister, Leah. Since it was tradition for the older sister to marry first, Laban saw his chance and took it. Ironically, Jacob didn't realize this until the next day, which begs a few questions that I'm not going to try to answer right now. (See chapter 1 about the wedding potentially being a banger of a party, which I assume contributed to the whoopsie.)

Well, now we have a predicament: seven years down the drain and a wife he didn't want. What shall we do? I know! Make another deal with Uncle Laban. Jacob agreed to work another seven years to marry Rachel, but he didn't have to wait. Rachel would become his wife in a week (happy honeymoon, Leah!), but he would stay on for the remainder of the years he owed.

Life got awkward as Rachel and Leah settled in with Jacob, and an interesting pattern emerged: Even though Rachel was the one Jacob loved, she wasn't able to have a baby. She was beautiful and favored, but she was infertile and therefore considered less-than.

For years, Rachel watched Leah deliver babies while her womb remained empty. At one point she even made a subtle suggestion to her hubby: "Give me children or I will die." Sweet gal.

Not only is she devastated that she can't provide a child for her husband, she is living alongside her sister and *her* seven children. Not only is it "I can't have children," but even worse, "I can't have children, but she can."

But she can.

And there it is: the three words that run through your mind countless times a day. So many times, in fact, that it keeps you from thinking of the things you do have.

What's heartbreaking about Rachel and Leah's story is that they were both trapped in a comparison prison of their own making, each focusing so intently on what the other had that they couldn't appreciate their own blessings. Rachel had Jacob's love—the thing almost every woman in that culture desperately wanted—but she couldn't enjoy it because she was consumed by Leah's fertility. Leah had children—the ultimate blessing and security for women in that time—but she couldn't celebrate them because she was desperate for Jacob's affection.

Each sister was living with a constant reminder of what she lacked. Every time Rachel saw Leah's children, it was evidence that she was failing at the most fundamental aspect of womanhood. Every time Leah saw Jacob's tenderness toward Rachel, it confirmed her worst fear: that she was unlovable. They were stuck in the same house, raising children together, sharing a husband, but unable to find contentment because they were measuring their worth against each other instead of recognizing their own unique gifts.

You Are Not Forgotten

This is exactly what comparison does to us: It blinds us to our blessings by keeping our eyes fixed on someone else's. Rachel couldn't see that being deeply loved was a rare and beautiful gift because she was too busy staring at Leah's children. Leah couldn't celebrate the miracle of life growing in her womb because she was too focused on the love that seemed reserved for her sister.

The tragedy is that each woman had something beautiful and significant, but comparison made them both feel like failures. They spent years feeling inadequate and jealous when they could have spent those same years grateful for the different but equally valuable gifts they'd been given.

We pound our fists instead of paying attention, and we miss it.

Envy morphs into entitlement, and before we know it, we've decided not only that we want something but that we deserve it. She's a jerk—why did she get the backyard pool? Incidentally, there is a real person on social media who I am basing that whole bikini/pool story on, and much to my chagrin, she seems like a delightful person who spends most of her time talking about how grateful she is for her life.

Want to know how awful I am? Instead of immediately thinking of how wonderful it is that she lives a grateful life, I think, *I'd talk about it all the time if I had your life too.*

I know it's not her whole life, but because it's all I see, I have no way to imagine the rest.

When we start going down this path of thinking, we also turn out to be the kind of people who celebrate the downfall of others because it means we're better than them.

We will never be content until we move from horizontal comparison to vertical contentment.

We see this as we watch the progression of names Leah gives her children. Her first three sons had names that reflected her desperate hope that having children would finally make Jacob love her: Reuben ("Surely my husband will love me now"), Simeon ("The Lord heard that I am not loved"), Levi ("Now my husband will become attached to me"). When she had her fourth son, she moved away from what was missing in her life and focused on the spectacular truth.

Judah's name means "This time I will praise the Lord." I will praise the Lord for the beautiful things He has given me instead of holding them up against other people before I decide how much I should value them.

Scripture says that after years of infertility, God remembered Rachel, listened to her, and opened up her womb. For clarification, He hadn't forgotten her. He didn't miss the request. He wasn't just focused on Leah and all her children.

It doesn't mean it can't feel that way, though.

So what does it mean that He "remembered" her?

It means God acted on her behalf at the exact moment He was always going to act.

The delay was by design—it wasn't an indication of her insignificance.

This concept of God's timing being by design rather than neglect is crucial for those of us trapped in comparison cycles. When we see others getting what we've been praying for—the promotion, the relationship, the healing, the breakthrough—it's easy to believe that God has forgotten us or that we're somehow less deserving of His attention.

But Rachel's story teaches us that God's delays aren't signs of His indifference or forgetfulness. He wasn't busy blessing Leah while Rachel slipped His mind. This wasn't about having a favorite or not caring about a desire.

Sometimes God's timing serves purposes we can't see in the moment. Maybe the delay was preparing Rachel's heart for motherhood in a way that immediate success wouldn't have. Maybe it was positioning her son Joseph to be born at exactly the right time for the role he would later play in saving his family, the nation of Egypt, and God's people. Maybe it was teaching both sisters to depend on God rather than on their circumstances for their identity and worth.

The delay doesn't mean you're forgotten. It means you're loved enough to receive God's best timing rather than your preferred timing.

And boy, did God come through when He gave Rachel

her first son. You may remember Joseph as the fashion icon who liked to flash his fancy rainbow coat and tell his brothers they were going to bow down to him. If we had more time, I would tell you about how they put him in a well, sold him to strangers, and smeared blood on his pretty jacket to convince his dad, Jacob, he was dead.

It's the age-old story: Comparison can get you thrown in a well.

If I had even more time than that, I would tell you that Joseph eventually became one of the most significant men in the Old Testament and that his life bore witness to the God who remembered his mother.

It might not have been the way she would have written it, but then again, it was already written perfectly—she just couldn't see it yet. Actually, she never saw it, because she died giving birth to her next son, but let's skip that part for the sake of my strong and inspirational closing.

You are not a guest star in someone else's movie, and you aren't a forgotten character in yours.

The God who remembered Rachel remembers you, and the desires of your heart are safe in His hands.

You're a masterpiece, friend, and your life is a testament to His wild love. Not a single part of your life is accidental, and not a moment is missed by your Father in heaven. You are covered, cared for, and beloved by the One who spun you into being and has never forgotten the desires of your heart. I pray you believe that a little more every day.

A Benediction for Comparison Junkies

I pray that you do not judge your wins by the wins of others and that you don't feel passed over when it seems God has forgotten the desires of your heart. May you not slip into a life of bitterness or envy, but may you look to Him when you're tempted to look at others. When you look in the mirror, may you see more of Jesus than yourself, and when you feel abandoned, may you feel His arms around you.

May you learn the joy that comes from a true relationship with your Father, who does everything for your good even when it feels like He doesn't care. I pray that the lies of the world will be silenced and that you will know that in Him, you are enough.

4

No-Hustle Zone

You are valuable.

Busyness is an illness of the spirit.
EUGENE PETERSON

I am no longer comfortable denying a fact about myself that everyone else seems to have known about me for years. Much to my surprise, the pattern of being chronically late is somehow my fault. I'll tell you how it happens so you can see my side of things, and then maybe you'll understand why the whole "I'm 99 percent sure it's the rest of the world" theory has not been ruled out.

I will watch the clock, convince myself I can get ready in about half the time it will actually take me, and put it off until ten minutes after I should have left, because it's not my fault I had things to stare at. Because I am a thoughtful person, I will let people know I will be late. That is the way I give back, even though it is their fault this particular time was chosen because I had things not to do.

This way of thinking has led to a few harrowing experiences with moms who "make their own food to bring to potluck events" and "get their kids to events when they are supposed to be there." Grocery store cookies on a plate (plastic wrap included, if you've left a window of prep time) are my contribution of choice. Even more stressful than potlucks or meetings with rigid start times is the twelve-year-old daughter who somehow left my body with a highlighter in one hand and a pouch of punctuality in the other.

Let me tell you a fun story about bonding with her before a friend's birthday party.

I will begin this tale with an unlikely and yet true fact: We left with plenty of time to spare. I knew where we were stopping, the gift we were picking up, and the traffic patterns for the greater Nashville area. As far as who gave me this information, I plead the fifth. Irrelevant.

What I didn't know was that it was tax-free weekend and Target had set up roller-coaster queues that were hovering dangerously close to the Magnolia section, which as you undoubtedly know, has since shifted because of the great and terrible remodel. The best thing to come from that was cup holders in the carts, but I guess I'm still confused about why that was a revolutionary thought in the year of our Lord 2019.

I digress. We can come back to the dark days of the prairie dress revival some other time.

Charlotte prefers to be at least fifteen minutes early (or a month, if we're talking about birth). Let me be clear: She sets her alarm two full hours before she needs to leave for school so she can practice basketball, take a shower, make breakfast, and have a generous thirty minutes for her skin routine.

She is twelve years old, and about a year ago, I opened her bedroom door at 6:15 a.m. to find her in downward dog with a video of wake-up stretches playing on Todd's computer. Another day I walked out to the kitchen, where she was perched on the edge of a chair, steaming decaf cupped in her hands while she stared wistfully out the window, undoubtedly contemplating the riddles of life.

Her seventeen-year-old sister, Kate, has a different philosophy on life: *I will get there when I get there, and your life will be better when I arrive.* In a twisted and cruel turn of events, she drives Charlotte to school now. That has been nothing short of *great joy* for everyone involved. Lucky for Kate, she gets a wake-up visit and at least two more check-ins before Charlotte ends up on the front bench with her backpack on, screaming upstairs in desperation and judgment. I empathize with Kate because she wasn't at the meeting where they chose when the school bell rang, so it's not exactly her problem.

Back to the wonders of Target: We grabbed the marshmallow toy thing (I don't know), a card, and a gift bag and began the trek to the beeping in the promised land. We were approximately five guests away when another register opened and there was a mass exodus. Chaos ensued. It was every woman for herself now. I decided to stay where I was because I understand Murphy's law, and moving would only bring me heartbreak. This happened before I realized that the next person in my line was playing a fun game of "how many things can I find that do not have a shred of identifying information."

And now I was ticked and hot and doing everything I could not to remind her what we both know: She has no right to shop there like a regular human. I grabbed a magazine and flipped through it because celebrity gossip is the kind of distraction I used to pay for before they went from a $1.99 purchase to a third of my mortgage.

I was finally next in line. Charlotte was pacing and initiating adoption negotiations with a woman who seemed keto-ish, and the woman ahead of me was lowering her items onto the belt like they were legacy china. Charlotte asked for my phone and started doing the side-to-side rocking thing that indicated she was entering the funnel that ends with her walking into the party asking if it looks like she'd been crying.

We had ten minutes to get there—which is plenty of time to drive twenty minutes.

And (I can't make this up) there was construction, and as the time hit one o'clock, we both started to tear up. I was apologizing and she was begging me to hurry and I was the worst mom and I hated everyone and everything that had done this to me. "I left early," I told her. "Remember? We left early. None of this is my fault."

We showed up at the party venue fifteen minutes late, both of us flushed and on edge. It was one of those "Mom has to stay so this is not a break for you" kinds of events, because good moms like that kind of thing. I set the gift down as Charlotte got her wristband. I apologized profusely and was tempted to go into great detail about all the obstacles that stood in the way of me making it to Olivia's life-defining twelfth birthday party, but I resisted because these are the excuses of women without Crock-Pots.

Within the span of ten minutes, I cried in the bathroom, found a metal bench to sit on outside while the splotches faded, and replayed the whole expedition until I felt the kind of guilt that tangles you up inside.

I turned around, my eyes squinting through the glass to make sure she was okay, but she was nowhere to be found. Her friends were sliding down inflatables and jumping into splits on a trampoline, and mine had probably sidled up next to whichever mom looks the most like a therapist.

It turns out I couldn't see her because she was climbing up to take her turn on the slide. She was giggling with friends, completely recovered from the trauma I had inflicted.

What scared me wasn't just that I'd stressed her out—it was that I was teaching her my relationship with time. That somehow urgency equals importance and being late means disappointing people. I don't want her to inherit my belief that the clock gets to decide whether we're good enough. I was modeling what it looks like when your heart is constantly divided between where you are and where you think you should be.

I hate that she was upset and that I was the cause of her stress, but what is true of that situation is true of many others in our lives: We treat everyday inconveniences like they are urgent, and it's taking a toll on our bodies. We live in constant fight-or-flight mode, always jumping to the next thing but never catching up.

The Toll of Chronic Busyness

Your body can't tell the difference between being at gunpoint and running late to a party, so it exhausts itself daily. When we live in chronic hurry mode, our nervous systems are constantly activated, as if we're facing actual danger. Our heart rate increases, our cortisol levels spike, our muscles tense up, and our breathing becomes shallow—all because the checkout line is moving too slowly.

This chronic stress response wreaks havoc on our physical health in ways we don't often connect to our hurried lifestyle. Constantly elevated cortisol levels suppress the immune system, disrupt sleep, and contribute to anxiety and depression. Digestion suffers because our bodies aren't designed to process food while in fight-or-flight mode. We develop headaches, muscle tension, and that constant feeling of being wired but tired.

The emotional toll is just as devastating. When everything feels urgent, nothing feels special. We rush through conversations with our kids, speed through meals, and hurry past moments of beauty because we're always mentally three steps ahead of where we actually are. We become emotionally unavailable even when we're physically present, always divided between the moment we're in and the next thing on our list.

Maybe most tragically, chronic hurry makes us spiritually deaf. We miss the gentle nudges from God because we're too busy managing our own agenda. We blow past divine appointments because they don't fit into our schedule. We pray rushed prayers and hurry through devotionals and wonder why we feel disconnected from the God who is trying to meet us in the margins of our overstuffed days.

Our children absorb all this tension. They learn that love is expressed through efficiency, that relationships are secondary to schedules, and that their worth is measured by how little inconvenience they cause the adults around them. We're raising a generation of kids who think normal life is supposed to feel like an emergency.

We pack our schedules because it's become increasingly difficult to stop running. Busyness is a status symbol these days—it says we matter and we have a lot of important things to do and important people to see. It means our kids are part of things and we are needed and in demand. It means we are someone to somebody, and we wear that badge of honor like a hard-earned battle scar.

This shift is relatively recent in human history. Our grandparents' generation viewed leisure as a sign of success—if you could afford to take your time, enjoying long meals and unhurried conversations, it meant you'd made it. But somewhere along the way, we flipped the script. Now being busy means you're important, sought after, valuable. Having a packed calendar has become proof of your worth.

We've created a culture where saying "I'm so busy" is both a complaint and a humble-brag. We compete over who has the most packed schedule, whose kids have the most activities, who gets the least sleep because they have so many commitments. We wear our exhaustion like a merit badge, as if being overwhelmed is evidence of how much we matter.

Social media has amplified this pressure exponentially. Everyone else seems to be crushing their goals, attending amazing events, and living their best life at lightning speed. The fear of missing out drives us to say yes to everything, as if a full calendar is the only defense against being forgotten or left behind.

But here's what we don't talk about: Much of our busyness is actually avoidance in disguise. When we're constantly moving, we don't have to sit with uncomfortable feelings or face difficult questions about what we really want from life. When every minute is scheduled, we don't have to wrestle with boredom, loneliness, or the existential anxiety that comes with stillness. Busyness becomes a drug that numbs us to the deeper longings of our souls.

It doesn't have to be this way—there's another way that leads to rest and freedom, and I have a feeling it's going to rattle you in a beautiful way.

It's Not About Doing More

Chronic busyness isn't a scheduling issue; it's a coping strategy.

We've trained our minds to be so "efficient" with our time that taking a break seems irresponsible and lazy.

So it's no wonder we've learned to feel chronically behind even when we don't know what's ahead. Most of the time we don't even have that much to do; it's just that our minds have learned that constant productivity is the norm.

The solution isn't to clear your calendar; it's to stop letting it run your life. When we're constantly rushing, we miss the gentle nudges, the unexpected conversations, the moments when God is trying to redirect our attention. Hurry-sickness doesn't just exhaust our bodies—it disconnects us from the very presence we're designed to live in.

Don't miss the appointments you didn't realize you had because you are so consumed with the ones you've made.

Often the most powerful question we can ask is, "Lord, where do You want me to do Your work today?"

This isn't about doing more or doing different things—it's about doing whatever you're already doing with a different heart. Your calendar might stay the same, but your perspective will completely change. You will cultivate a spirit of open-handedness when it comes to your to-do list. What you once saw as inconveniences will be reshaped into purposeful conversations and events. At the end of the day, it isn't necessarily that your hands were too busy. Your heart, however, is a different story. What if the answer isn't to change your commitments but to be more present for what you're already doing?

As you consider your schedule for the week ahead, here are some things to keep in mind.

Check for divine appointments.

Before rushing out the door or hurrying someone along, ask, "Lord, is there something You want me to notice here that

I'm about to miss?" Sometimes it's your child needing to tell you about something that happened at school. Sometimes it's the neighbor who's outside and looks like she needs to talk. Sometimes it's absolutely nothing and you really do just need to go. But asking the question changes your posture from "Everything is urgent" to "What actually matters right now?"

Examine your inherited pace.

This one hits deep: Examine what you learned about time and urgency from your family of origin. Many of us inherited scripts about being constantly late or believing that being on time equals being worthy of love and acceptance. When you realize you're passing on this same anxiety to your kids, it's easier to consciously break the cycle. Practice saying things like "We have time to do this well" instead of "Hurry up!"

Reframe the delays.

Instead of automatically saying, "We're running behind!" when something slows you down, practice saying, "God, what are You wanting me to learn about trust right now?" It sounds cheesy, but it literally rewires your brain to see delays as opportunities for patience rather than evidence that your day is ruined. Instead of catastrophizing delays ("This ruins everything!"), you're looking for meaning or growth opportunities in stressful situations. Sometimes the lesson is just "Traffic exists and it's not personal."

Notice what you're rushing through.

Before bed, ask: "What did I rush through today that I wish I'd savored?" This helps you see where you're choosing mental chaos over being fully present. The things you chronically rush through reveal where you could practice depth instead of speed. Are you always rushing through bedtime routines? Morning coffee? Conversations with your spouse? When we're constantly rushing, we get so focused on what's next that we can't enjoy what's now.

The goal isn't to eliminate all sense of urgency from your life—sometimes things genuinely are time sensitive. The goal is to develop the discernment to know the difference between actual urgency and manufactured urgency, between godly productivity and anxious busyness.

This kind of mindful presence takes practice and the ability to know when we are busy with the wrong things.

Choosing the Better Portion

Here are two ladies who barely need an introduction. "Put your hands together for Mary and Maaaaaaarrrrthhhhaaaaa!"

They were sisters who called Jesus a friend. They had another sibling you might have heard of because of his whole "back from the dead" origin story. You guessed it: Lazarus!

Mary and Martha's Story

For more about the story of Mary and Martha and their struggle to choose the better portion, see Luke 10:38-42.

In case you aren't familiar with these siblings, I'll give you a quick summary as we begin their story. They were hosting a get-together at their house when Jesus came to speak to the people gathered there. Mary took a seat in the front row and was hanging on every word the Lord was saying, wholly focused on the moment with Jesus. Martha, on the other hand, was in the kitchen whipping up some food, and she was clearly annoyed that Mary wasn't helping her. So much so that she tattled to the living God.

"She's not helping me. She's just sitting there. Tell her to get up and stop being lazy!"

At this point, Jesus told her not to worry about Mary because she was doing the right thing.

Like, let the shish kebabs marinate, girl. They didn't come here for your grandma's pudding recipe.

So Mary was doing the right thing and Martha wasn't.

Well . . . that's a version you might have heard, but it doesn't tell the whole story.

Almost invariably, the word *rebuked* is used when this story is told, but Scripture doesn't say that. In fact, I don't think this conversation has anything to do with what Martha was working on. He never told her she was doing something wrong, and He never told her to stop or go sit with her sister.

What He was rebuking was the idea that Mary was doing something lazy instead of what she was supposed to be doing. Like, why are you such a tattletale, Martha? #firstborn. I'm actually not 100 percent sure she was the eldest, but she's definitely got the vibe down.

Scripture describes Martha as distracted, anxious, and troubled—basically, her mind was being pulled in a million directions, with way too much internal noise.

Jesus wasn't speaking about what her hands were doing; He was speaking to what her mind was doing. So if we were to look at the descriptive words, Martha = anxious and Mary = focused on the portion that matters.

Here's what's fascinating: The word for "anxious" actually comes from the same root as "portion." So Mary chose one thing to focus on, while Martha was trying to focus on everything at once. Mary's mind was centered, and Martha's was scattered all over the place. Essentially, the Lord was saying, "You can either choose the right part or be torn apart."

Our lives are busy. We are going to hurry. Incidentally, that's not always a bad thing.

What we can do, however, is cultivate the mentality of Mary while working like Martha.

It's easy to misunderstand Scripture if we take it out of its original context, so let me add a little bit of detail here. It was culturally appropriate to be doing what Martha was doing. Even more than that, women were judged on how well they served their guests. It wasn't an option—it was their responsibility and the expectation of everyone present. Martha wasn't being selfish or showing off—she was doing exactly what society expected of a good hostess.

On the other hand, it was not only countercultural but likely offensive that Mary had chosen to sit at the feet of Jesus. That was a place reserved for the disciples of rabbis—for men.

And what did Jesus do? He told Martha (and everyone else who was present) that her sister was exactly where she should be. He went on to say that it wouldn't be taken from her. She was welcome to be there as a disciple alongside the men.

Here's what was revolutionary about this story: Jesus wasn't saying that Martha's work didn't matter. He was saying that Mary's choice to prioritize learning and relationship over cultural expectations was the "better portion" that wouldn't be taken away. Both sisters were busy—one with the business of hospitality, the other with the business of discipleship.

The difference wasn't in their activity level; it was in their focus. Martha was doing many necessary things, but her mind was scattered, anxious, and resentful. Mary was doing one thing—listening to Jesus—and her attention was completely absorbed in what mattered most. Martha was multitasking; Mary was single-tasking.

This is what it means to be "busy with the business of Jesus" in our own lives. It's not about stopping all productive activity and sitting in perpetual meditation. It's about doing whatever we're doing with undivided attention and a heart that's anchored in what matters most. You can change diapers with the focus of Mary. You can attend meetings with the posture of a disciple. You can grocery shop with a spirit that's listening for God's voice.

The goal isn't to eliminate Martha's work—we need people who prepare meals and organize events and take care of practical details. The goal is to do Martha's work with Mary's heart:

focused, present, and rooted in what truly matters, rather than scattered by anxiety about everything that needs to be done.

Life is going to continue to happen.

Mary didn't just go into a trance and have an otherworldly experience where the reality around her disappeared and she was somehow able to shut it out completely.

Guess what? Even when the King of the world was fingertips away, she still faced distractions. Maybe she noticed His stubble, wondered if He was hungry, or got annoyed at the guy who kept raising his hand with questions.

If you ever start to feel bad that your life keeps happening, think about how people who could physically touch Jesus eventually left the room because they had other things to do and places to be.

"This has been great. Took a lot of notes and really connected with the stuff about the poor. The wife is going to kill me if I'm not back in time to put the kids down. Martha, killer pudding as usual."

Think about that for a minute. Every single person in that room, even those listening intently, was still aware of and engaged with the environment they were in and the thoughts going through their mind. No matter how hard they tried, it was impossible to forget that it all existed. We only know God in the context of this world, and that isn't going to change.

I would imagine that at some point over the course of Martha and Mary's dinner party, there was a conversation about something other than Jesus. If you're anything like me, you forget this when you read Bible stories. You freeze them in your mind, and they exist in a particular scene, but you don't necessarily think about how they were normal people like us. Maybe there were two men in the room who hadn't spoken for years because of a disagreement, and in the back of their minds, they were trying to avoid each other. Someone might have been desperately sad over a breakup or self-conscious that his tunic wasn't the latest fashion.

The world was a distraction even when He was in their midst—it still took intentionality to stay grounded in what was most important.

People still had to make the decision to be intentional about their time with Jesus.

Here's the truth about chronic hurrying: It's more about being internally divided than it is about our actions. The reason we're so overwhelmed with our schedules isn't really because we have places to be; it's that our minds are always pulled in different directions. We have to remember where our center is and let the spokes be driven from that.

You can be in traffic or attending practice and still have a posture of attentiveness to the Spirit of God. You can be unloading the dishwasher and remember that the Rabbi is still teaching.

Thousands of years have passed, but the truth remains: He is always in the room.

Rabbi, teach us to sit at Your feet no matter where ours are.

A Benediction for the Busy

In a world of rushing and being half-present, may your body and your heart slow to a new rhythm of grace. I pray that in the moments you feel yourself panicked for time and overwhelmed with obligations, you will remember that these moments do not define your life or your identity. May you be courageously countercultural and mindful of what your "one thing" is at any given moment.

May the soft, steady pace of true life with Jesus become second nature and the hum of the world be hushed along the way.

5

Nothing to Prove

You are enough.

Perfectionism is the voice of the oppressor; the enemy of the people. It will keep you insane your whole life.

ANNE LAMOTT

I can think of few things people judge you more harshly for than parenting, which is why I decided to do it perfectly.

Let me introduce you to a lady named Astentine. She isn't exactly a person, but more of a plastic head with hair. She was an Amazon purchase that is typically made by people in hair school, but here we are.

She had clamps that tightened her to the table so you could practice different hairstyles. But she still wobbled, which led Charlotte to eventually name her Astentine, because she looked up words that meant "unstable" and apparently this was one of them. I just googled it to make sure I was spelling it right, and it turns out it was supposed to be *astatine*. We never even called her by the right name, and as you will see, she also suffered a horrible end.

Anyway, the reason she came to our house was because I could not figure out how to make French braids as perfectly as other moms, despite getting some hands-on mentoring and watching every YouTube video created since the dawn of digital time. My children were whiners who didn't want me to practice on them for three hours at a time because they wanted to have their own lives, so you can see what put me in this predicament.

When I say I get obsessed with things, I mean that I will stop if a hair is out of place. I am determined to get it exactly right, and what started out as a fun parenting jaunt turned into what might be considered an unhealthy commitment to inconsequential results.

When I fold sheets, they have to be the exact same size. The lengths I have gone to achieve this would impress and terrify you, but suffice it to say that at one point I embroidered tiny stars to color-coordinate sets and identify exactly where the folds needed to be to line up.

I am the same person who will leave a load of laundry sitting for weeks and typically has some kind of old drink next to dried-up contacts on my nightstand, so the whole adventure is a little willy-nilly.

Astentine did not live a long life because the neighborhood kids started hiding her all over the house to scare people, and then they gave her a series of haircuts that ended with her looking like the little girl from *Finding Nemo*. She was laid to rest in a proper service and thrown into a trash bag, no doubt having one last hurrah with the garbage collectors.

My perfectionism shows up in strange ways—most of which are the product of determination. But there are other ways it shows up, and those are the ones I regret.

Honestly, some of my hardest moments have come in the wake of realizing I have done something that bruised my children's hearts.

There is a series of photographs that exists somewhere, although I don't look for them because I don't want to see them. It was fall, and I had made dresses for my girls—Ellie (the youngest) couldn't have been more than five. I had spent hours on them, even embroidering their names and finding matching bows.

I wanted to take pictures, and as I was getting them dressed, Ellie burst into tears. I have no recollection why, but I do remember it didn't stop me. I parted her hair perfectly and smoothed each side into perfect pigtails, with the ends twirled at the bottom, the way they always did. I moved on to Abby and Kate while Ellie continued to cry, which had now become a problem, because she had worked her way to gasping for air and her face had gone cherry red.

What I recall is that I was more concerned with the photos than whatever was upsetting her, and I'm sure I told her so, even if it wasn't in words. I dragged the girls out to the front porch and sat them side by side as the sun hit exactly where I wanted it to be.

It wasn't until later that I looked back at the images and saw Ellie's tiny face, swollen, red eyed, and sweaty. It was her smile that killed me. She had forced it, and it was very clear that she was trying the best she could to do what I was asking of her.

Your job is to meet my needs even if it hurts.

You need to help me create this moment because I need it to be perfect.

This was years and years before social media—it was just a broken moment between a child who wanted to please her mother and a mother who made her think she had to.

I don't need to find the pictures to remember her smile perfectly—some moments of failure are carved into us so deeply that we see them without the evidence.

What strikes me about both of these stories—Astentine and the photo shoot—is that they weren't really about hair braids or perfect pictures at all. They were about something much more primal: the terror that if I didn't get it exactly right, it would mean something devastating about who I am as a person.

The hair braids weren't just hair braids—they were proof that I was the kind of mother who cared enough to master Pinterest-worthy skills. The photo shoot wasn't just about capturing a moment—it was about creating evidence that I had beautiful, well-dressed children and therefore must be doing something right. In both cases, I was trying to manufacture worthiness through flawless execution.

Perfectionism isn't about high standards or attention to detail. It's about believing that our value as human beings is directly tied to our ability to perform without failure. It's the exhausting conviction that we are always one mistake away from being exposed as frauds, disappointing the people we love, or—most terrifyingly—losing God's approval.

Perfectionism makes grace feel dangerous—like it could be pulled out from under us at any moment.

You Are More Than What You Do

The idea of failing may feel catastrophic to us because, from our earliest years, we were raised in homes where worth was tied to performance. Love wasn't given freely; it was earned by grades, behavior, or compliance. We learned early: Do it right and you're safe; do it wrong and you're exposed. That belief doesn't evaporate when we grow up—it solidifies.

We aren't afraid of the mistake itself—we're afraid of what the mistake means. When something goes wrong, we hear, *You're incompetent. You're unwanted. You're an impostor. You're a never-was, a never-will-be.*

We become convinced that others are hyperfocused on what we see as our weaknesses. Someone teases you lightly, and what they mean as affection lands like judgment. Someone forgets to say thank you, and suddenly silence sounds like proof of failure.

For me, the fear of failure shows up in little things. I can be absent-minded, and more than once I've convinced myself that forgetting to turn in papers means I don't belong in a classroom. A coworker laughs kindly about me being scatterbrained, and my instinct is to smile along while quietly drafting the real story in my head. *See? They all think you're incompetent.*

What do I do? Overcompensate. I buy all the organizers and color-code things. I create systems to avoid being judged, while the truth is that they probably aren't paying as much attention as I think they are.

This is the side of perfectionism we don't talk about much. It isn't always obsessively rewriting emails or straightening picture frames. Sometimes it's the low-grade panic that every small mistake confirms your worst fear: *You are not enough.* The successes don't stick—they feel like temporary reprieves. But the failures? Those feel permanent.

Psychologists call this way of filtering reality *schemas.*[1] They're mental frameworks built in childhood that tell us who we have to be to stay safe or loved. *Don't mess up. Don't be needy. Don't be average.* These tapes run in the background of our minds all day, and because they're so familiar, they feel like truth instead of programming.

The cruel part is that failure screams louder than success. A win offers a sigh of relief, but a loss seems to prove the story we fear is true. So we keep striving, caught in a cycle where rest is impossible and grace feels like it's always one mistake away from running out.

Psychologists Paul Hewitt and Gordon Flett have studied perfectionism for decades, and they describe three main types.[2]

Self-oriented perfectionism is when the pressure comes from inside—you demand flawless results from yourself, no matter the cost. This is the voice that tells you one B on a test means you're a failure or one bad day at work means you don't belong.

Socially prescribed perfectionism is the belief that everyone else is silently measuring you, and you'll only be accepted if you're perfect. This is the panic that shows up when you think a late email or a forgotten paper confirms everyone's worst suspicions about you.

And then there's *other-oriented perfectionism*—holding people around you to impossible standards. That one stings to admit, because it's the version that can wound our families the most. It's when my need to create a perfect picture turned into a demand that my daughter smile through her tears.

As this framework shows, perfectionism isn't one-dimensional. It doesn't just live in our heads—it seeps into our relationships, our work, our parenting, our faith. And the more we chase it, the more it costs.

You can see where this goes spiritually. Instead of resting in grace, we live as though we're two steps away from losing it. Faith becomes more like a performance than a relationship, and we live with the constant suspicion that we're not quite enough.

Here's the hard truth: Perfectionism doesn't disappear because someone tells you to "stop being so hard on yourself." It only loosens its grip when you learn to name the lie underneath it and practice new ways of responding.

Loosening the Hold of Perfectionism

If you recognize areas of your life where perfectionism has a hold on you, there are some steps you can take to break that cycle.

Name the story, not just the mistake.

When you blow something, ask, *What story am I telling myself right now?* Forgetting a deadline doesn't actually equal *I'm incompetent*. That's the schema talking. Write down the chain: event → interpretation → identity. Often, seeing it on paper shows how exaggerated it is.

For example: "I was late to the meeting" becomes "I'm always disorganized" becomes "I'm the kind of person who can't handle responsibility." See how we jumped from one late arrival to a fundamental character flaw? The event was small, but the story we tell ourselves is devastating. Practice interrupting this chain by asking, *Is this actually about my character, or is this just a thing that happened?*

Measure process instead of outcome.

Perfectionists only grade themselves by results: A or F. But growth happens in the middle. Did you show up? Did you take a step? Did you practice faithfulness, even if it was clumsy? Shifting the metric recalibrates the inner scales.

Instead of saying, "Did I nail the presentation?" ask, "Did I prepare as well as I could with the time I had?" Instead of saying, "Was I the perfect parent today?" ask, "Did I show up with love, even when I was tired?" This isn't lowering your standards—it's measuring what's actually in your control.

Practice "good enough" decisions.

Pick one small area where you tend to overthink—maybe what to wear, which route to take, or what to order at a restaurant—and commit to making a choice within thirty seconds, without second-guessing. It sounds trivial, but perfectionism often shows up in these micromoments, and learning to be okay with "good enough" in small things builds the muscle for bigger decisions.

The goal isn't to become careless—it's to learn that most decisions aren't as consequential as your perfectionistic brain believes they are. When you catch yourself spending fifteen minutes choosing between two nearly identical options, set a timer for two minutes and make a choice. You're training yourself to trust that you can handle the consequences of imperfect decisions.

Practice deliberate imperfection.

Most perfectionism thrives in micromoments—an email, a meeting, a small presentation. One way to retrain your brain is to choose something small to leave imperfect, on purpose.

Psychologists call this "exposure with response prevention"—deliberately doing the thing that makes you anxious and resisting the urge to fix it.[3]

For a perfectionist, that might mean sending the email without rereading it twelve times. Or leaving the bows a little crooked on the gift. Or letting your child's project be their project, not your polished version. The point isn't to be careless—it's to build tolerance for imperfection.

And here's the spiritual side: It becomes a way of confessing, "I am not God. I don't hold the world together. My worth is not riding on this one flawless performance." Every small act of deliberate imperfection is a rebellion against the lie that you have to be flawless to be loved.

Reframe failure as data, not verdict.

Perfectionists interpret every mistake as evidence: *You're incompetent. You're not enough. You've been exposed.* But a healthier approach is to embrace a growth mindset—treating failure as information, not identity.

Here's how it looks in practice: When you fail, literally write it out in two columns. In one, the perfectionist verdict: "I forgot the paper—therefore I'm a terrible teacher." In the other, the data: "I forgot the paper—so I need a system to check my bag before leaving home." One column fuels shame; the other fuels growth.

Spiritually, this echoes what Paul writes in Romans: There is "no condemnation" for those in Christ. Condemnation says failure defines you; conviction says failure can redirect you. If you can reframe mistakes as data points rather than verdicts, you'll actually grow to be more resilient, creative, and free.

What do faithful steps look like in daily life? They're smaller than you think. It's sending the email even though it's not perfectly worded. It's volunteering for something you're not sure you're qualified for. It's having the conversation you've been avoiding because you don't know exactly what to say. It's showing up to serve even when you feel like you don't have much to offer.

I can't tell you how many times I've automatically disqualified myself from God's calling because I feel like I'm not the perfect candidate and I'll mess it up. I can back this up with countless examples of failures and weaknesses, and I'm always ready with an airtight speech if I'm put on the spot.

At the core of these excuses, I'm telling God that my ability to do things without failure is more important than trusting what He has laid out for me. I'm more concerned with doing things in a way that won't be judged than I am with being faithful in spite of my inadequacy.

I'm telling God that He isn't perfect enough to make up for my lack of perfection, and I spend more time thinking about how the world sees me than I do listening to Him declare who I am.

There has to be a better way, and as you might imagine, I have someone for you to meet.

The Strength You Have

I want you to say hello to our friend of the day: Gideon. As an Israelite, he and his people had been taken over by the Midianites (they were bad news bears and had been killing livestock, decimating land, and destroying crops). One day he was threshing wheat when an angel showed up.

> **Gideon's Story**
>
> *For more about Gideon and his story about letting go, see Judges 6–7.*

He was threshing this wheat in a strange place—a winepress, which would have been dug into the ground—in order to avoid danger from his enemies above.

The angel of the Lord greeted him by saying, "The Lord is with you, mighty warrior."

I'm sure Gideon was confused. He was not mighty, and he was certainly not a warrior. In fact, he was radically unqualified for either of those titles. Note that the angel did not say he was going to become a mighty warrior—this title was not dependent on Gideon doing a great job. It was declared over him as truth.

The angel gave him his assignment: "Go in the strength you have and save Israel out of Midian's hand. Am I not sending you?"

Notice what just happened here. God's message wasn't, "Go become a mighty warrior and then I'll use you." It was, "Go in the strength you have"—present tense. The strength Gideon already possessed, hiding in a winepress, threshing wheat in fear.

This is the opposite of how perfectionism works. Perfectionism says, "Get qualified first, then step forward." God says, "I'm calling you qualified right now. Let's go."

The strength you have.

Gideon bluntly told the angel that probably wasn't going to happen. He was the lowest in his family, and his family was the weakest clan in Manasseh.

You're going to need a guy who has authority and won't screw this up. I don't have the right background, so the assignment must be for someone else. Thanks for stopping by—now fly away to someone better.

Does this sound familiar? How many times have you talked yourself out of an opportunity because you focused on what you lacked rather than what God was offering?

Gideon's response is the perfectionist's default: immediate self-disqualification. He was the lowest in his family, his family was the weakest clan. But notice that God didn't argue with Gideon's assessment of his résumé—He simply redirected him to what actually mattered: "I will be with you."

I mean, Gideon didn't even listen to the assignment because he was too busy declining it.

But God's response was direct: "I will be with you, and you will strike down all the Midianites, leaving none alive." God gave him specific instructions: Start by tearing down the altar to Baal, and build one for Me.

To Gideon's credit, he did the renovating, but he did it at night because he was afraid of what his family and neighbors would think of him. It was a victory, which you may think would buoy his trust, but things were about to get more intense.

God called him to lead an army and kill all the Midianites, which sounds pretty reasonable, given that he's one guy threshing wheat.

Gideon kept asking for proof in all manner of wet and dry fleece, and God kept giving it. What strikes me most about the fleece part of the story isn't Gideon's insecurity—it's God's patience. Not once did He say, "That's it—you've asked too much, you're out." If I'm honest, that's what I expect sometimes—that God's grace has a limit, and my repeated failures will push Him over the edge. That's the false logic of perfectionism: One mistake too many, and you're disqualified.

But God doesn't operate that way. He didn't shrink back or remove His presence when Gideon faltered—He drew closer. That's the opposite of the pressure of perfectionism. Where perfectionism says, "You're tolerated as long as you perform," God says, "You're loved, and I'm not leaving."

That contrast is everything for me. Because most of my perfectionism has been fueled by fear—fear that failure will mean abandonment, fear that I'll finally reach the limit of grace. Gideon's story shows me that God's patience is longer than my fear.

Failure Isn't the End of the Story

This time Gideon knew God was talking to him, so he gathered up thirty-two thousand army members and started to plan. Surprisingly, through a series of somewhat odd events, God whittled this down to three hundred men.

God's message is clear: You are going to win, but it's not because you did it. It's because I did it and you chose to be obedient.

That's the part that stings for perfectionists. We prepare and perform, building our own "armies"—color-coded calendars, overstudying, obsessively reworking the email—because we think safety comes from stacking enough evidence that we won't fail. And then God starts shrinking the army. He lets the plans fall apart or the project go sideways—not because He enjoys watching us squirm but because He knows those things were never going to save us. The real test is whether we'll keep moving forward when the scaffolding is gone.

Here's what Gideon's story teaches us about perfectionism: God doesn't choose us because we're flawless—He chooses us so that when something extraordinary happens, it's clear it came from Him, not from our perfect execution.

Think about it: If God had chosen someone who was already a renowned warrior with a massive army and impeccable credentials, the victory would have been attributed to human strength and strategy. But when a scared guy hiding in a winepress defeats an entire army with three hundred men and some torches, there's no question where the power came from.

This is why perfectionism ends up working against God's purposes in our lives. When we insist on being fully qualified before we obey, we're essentially saying we want the credit. We want to be able to point to our competence, our preparation, our flawless execution as the reason things went well.

But what if going "in the strength you have" means showing up with your questions, your fears, and your inadequacies? For me, that looks like teaching the class even when I forgot the papers. For someone else, it might mean going to the job interview without the perfect résumé, or apologizing even though you don't have the exact words. It's saying yes to the invitation before you've figured out what you'll bring to the table. That's what faith looks like in real life: moving without the guarantee of flawless execution. There is no strategy, resource, or idea that will lead to flawless execution.

Gideon's might didn't come from his ability; it came from his obedience.

He didn't need to be stronger, braver, or smarter. He just needed to believe the One who called him a mighty warrior before he went to battle.

We can't wait until we feel qualified, and we can't let our failures define us.

You're going to fumble the ball. You're going to disappoint people. You're going to miss the meeting, say something ridiculous, and leave fleece in the night air to test the Lord.

And that's okay.

But here's what I don't want to forget: The porch photos, the stomach-tightening fear of mistakes, the fleeces on the ground—they're all different versions of the same story. Perfectionism whispers that failure is final, that one misstep will expose us, that we can't move forward until we've earned the title.

The problem with perfectionism is that it doesn't stop once you've succeeded. The win fades, and suddenly you're scrambling to prove yourself again. Gideon did it with fleeces. I do it with classrooms and porch pictures. The cycle is exhausting—but it isn't the story God is telling.

Maybe the question worth carrying is not "How can I do this without failing?" but "What would it look like to move forward even if I do?" Because failure isn't the end of the story. Sometimes it's the place where God meets us most clearly, and the only way we'll ever discover that is if we dare to step out before we feel ready.

That's what I need most—not more proof, not another fleece, not a flawless track record. Just the courage to go in the strength I already have, trusting the One who is with me.

A Benediction for Recovering Perfectionists

The Lord never asked you to be perfect, and if you try, you will end up exhausted, in body and soul. I pray that even in the moments you feel like you've failed, you will be reminded that your performance does not determine your worth.

May you give yourself the grace the Lord gives, and may you walk in full confidence, knowing that nothing you do or don't do can change His love.

6

It's Not Your Job to Keep Everyone Safe

You are set free.

I'll be ready for it to happen and that way it won't happen. It's a burden, being able to control situations with my hyper-vigilance, but it's my lot in life.

TINA FEY

My father used to love telling the story of how I shocked doctors when I was born. Evidently, when they laid me on my mom's stomach, I lifted up my head and looked around. I was born hypervigilant.

So much so that I was hospitalized at age three because doctors were concerned that my anxiety was causing an ulcer. I couldn't stay in bed at night because I was convinced that if I didn't check my baby sister's breathing, make sure the stove was turned off, and confirm that the front door was locked, someone in my family would die.

I learned early that safety lived on the other side of vigilance.

No matter how many times my parents put me in bed, I would find a way to sneak out and sit just outside the room where they were watching TV so I could secretly make sure they were okay.

When I was pregnant with our fourth daughter, we found out she couldn't live outside of my body and would pass away immediately after she was born, if not before.

The following months brought some of the hardest days of my life. I decided to carry my daughter as long as I could—she lived for two and a half hours after she was born and was a beautiful, redheaded, three pound and two ounce miracle.

But I couldn't save her. There was nothing I could do. I couldn't save my Audrey even though I was growing her. It is a feeling of helplessness that's hard to describe: No one should have to choose a burial plot while a baby is kicking in her stomach.

The following month, my eight-week-old nephew died of SIDS.

The little girl who used to sneak out of bed to listen to her baby sister could do nothing to rescue them.

A few years later, I gave birth to my daughter Charlotte, and I was consumed with fear. I needed to know she was breathing through the night, so I bought a special sensor pad for her crib that was supposed to notify parents if there was a problem.

Night after night, the alarm would go off, and I would run, sweaty-palmed, across the hall. I decided that one mat wasn't enough and went back for another one so her whole crib was covered. It didn't stop the problem—somehow she always found a way to scoot far enough into a corner that the sensors couldn't detect her breathing.

One night I was on my third panicked response to the alarm, and of course she was fine. I started to walk out, and somewhere in the night, I heard the voice of the Lord (not audibly, but I really wish that would happen to me) asking me how long I was going to do this.

How long, Angie?

How long will you trust everything the world offers instead of trusting Me?

I stood there for several minutes, recalling the pain I had been through years before. I knew at that moment I was at a crossroads: I could take Him at His word, or I could spend the rest of my life obsessing over everything that could go wrong.

I carried a relentless belief that I had to be hypervigilant to the situations and people around me or things would fall apart. Of course, the times they did fall apart only convinced me I was right. We live in a world that constantly tells us that if we stay vigilant enough, everything will be fine.

Now I can track the speed my daughter is driving in real time—it's supposed to give me peace of mind, but it honestly fuels more anxiety. The more informed we are, the more we feel responsible for everything that might go wrong.

I miss the good ol' days.

When I was in middle school we had two corded phones in our house, which meant that if my friends called, I had to stretch the cord to a place where I could be behind a closed door. If I was on the phone (wait for it), I would have no idea if anyone else was trying to call. Later, we got wireless phones and call waiting, and I remember thinking technology could literally never get more sophisticated.

As someone who has lived through both the pre-smartphone era and the era of perpetual connectedness, I can tell you how much I wish we could go back to the way it used to be. It truly was so much simpler, but kids don't understand a world where you can't connect with a person the moment you want to. If my mother was picking me up at the mall at 5:00 and I sat out there for an hour waiting, I would have no way to call to see where she was (unless I used this special box called a pay phone, and that only worked if she was at home and I had a quarter). There was no GPS to check, no texting for an ETA—just waiting, wondering, and hoping everything was okay.

Also, Blockbuster.

These kids don't understand the feeling of running to the back of the store to see if one of the new movies had a plastic case behind the cover. If not, we would hustle back to the front to see if it had been put in the "returned" pile and hadn't made it back on the shelf yet.

They don't know a world where everything isn't at their fingertips. These kids don't know a world where you had to trust without knowing. But somehow, in gaining the ability to know everything, we've lost the ability to rest in anything.

Who's in Charge Here?

Vigilance is a lesson we learned early, and for many people, it was never a choice—it was how we survived. We learned to read a room before we could read a book. We noticed mood shifts, slammed doors, sighs, silences. We figured out how to adapt ourselves to avoid disaster.

When a child lives in a state of constant vigilance, these patterns become so deeply ingrained that they feel automatic as adults. The pathways your brain carved out to scan for threats became your default setting, which is why it's so hard to "just relax," even when you know you're safe.

These patterns don't just affect how we respond to real emergencies. They shape how we move through ordinary moments. You walk into your house and immediately scan for what needs to be done, what's out of place, who might need something. You can't sit down to watch a movie without mentally running through tomorrow's schedule. You attend your child's soccer game but spend half the time monitoring the weather, calculating drive times, and making contingency plans for every possible scenario.

The hypervigilant child becomes the hypervigilant adult who checks the locks three times, refreshes email compulsively, and lies awake running through everything that could go wrong tomorrow. You've never learned to trust that things might be okay without your constant supervision.

Maybe your parents fought, and you learned to gauge the tension in the house before you asked for help with homework. Maybe addiction lived in your home, and you became responsible for monitoring someone else's sobriety. Maybe mental illness meant you never knew which version of a parent you'd encounter, so you learned to read the signs and adjust accordingly. Maybe financial instability meant you learned to watch your parents' faces before asking for anything that cost money.

These weren't choices you made—they were adaptations you developed to survive in an environment that required a constant assessment of safety. The problem is that your nervous system doesn't know the difference between the chaos you grew up in and the stable life you've built as an adult. It keeps scanning for threats that no longer exist, keeps you alert for dangers that have passed.

The irony is that the very skill that protected you as a child—your ability to read situations and people with remarkable accuracy—can become a prison as an adult. You're so good at sensing what others need that you can't stop yourself from trying to meet those needs. You're so attuned to potential problems that you can't rest when things are actually going well.

Whether vigilance was born from necessity or learned as a survival strategy, technology has found a way to amplify whatever patterns we already had. The three-year-old who couldn't sleep until she checked on everyone has grown up in a world that never stops asking her to check on everyone. The child who learned to scan for danger now carries a device that provides endless opportunities to scan. Technology didn't create our vigilance—it just gave it superpowers.

And here's what makes it particularly insidious: Technology doesn't feel like vigilance. It feels like connection, productivity, being a good parent or friend. When you check your teenager's location for the fifth time today, it doesn't feel like anxiety—it feels like love. When you monitor your work email at 10 p.m., it doesn't feel like compulsion—it feels responsible. When you refresh social media to see what everyone's up to, it doesn't feel like surveillance—it feels like staying connected. The technology that was designed to make us feel more secure has made us more anxious.

Consider what happens in your body when you haven't checked your phone for an hour. Your heart rate increases slightly. Your shoulders tense. You start creating stories about what you might have missed. This isn't just in your head—research shows that people experience measurable withdrawal symptoms when separated from their devices. Your stress hormones increase. Your focus decreases. You become irritable and restless.

We were created to find security in a God who is everywhere, knows everything, and can do anything. We reach for god-powers without saying it out loud. Omnipresent: always reachable, always watching the dots on a map. Omniscient: researching every symptom, reading every review, knowing every ETA. Omnipotent: believing if I monitor the situation enough, nothing bad will happen. But hypervigilance isn't power—it's the denial that I don't have any.

But here's the cruel irony: Technology doesn't make you more in control; it makes you more aware of how little you are actually in control. It's informed helplessness—knowing exactly what's happening while being unable to do anything about it. You can watch your daughter's location on your phone and see that she's stuck in traffic, but you can't make the cars move. You can read about every possible side effect of your medication, but you can't guarantee you won't experience them. You have access to more information than any generation in history, yet you feel more anxious and powerless than ever.

Your brain receives the information as evidence that something could go wrong, but you still can't do anything to prevent it. It's like being forced to watch a movie where you can see the danger coming but can't warn the characters.

This is worse than obliviousness. When you didn't know, you could assume everything was fine. Now you know too much, and most of what you know only confirms how little influence you have over the outcomes that matter most.

We've lost the ability to tolerate not knowing anything. We can't even drive somewhere without GPS because the anxiety of being uncertain about directions feels unbearable. We can't wait for test results without googling every possible diagnosis. We can't let our teenagers go to a party without tracking their location. The discomfort of uncertainty has become so intolerable that we'd rather live in a state of informed anxiety than peaceful ignorance.

This shows up in the smallest moments of our days, in ways we don't even notice.

How do you feel if you haven't looked at your phone for

a few hours? (Take note if that sentence seemed ridiculous because you would never be away from it that long.)

As absurd as it may sound, when I see a message someone sent, my brain creates a movie that shows them staring at their phone and doing nothing else until I respond. *Oh my gosh, she has been FROZEN FOR THREE HOURS. She probably thinks I'm mad. Or maybe she's worried I'm thinking through my response or talking to other people about her.*

Ninety-nine percent of the time none of these things are happening.

Here's another reason I constantly check in with my texts: I don't want to open my phone or email and have ten million things to do. I imagine the list piling up and have anxiety over something that doesn't exist.

As someone who gets really edgy when I feel like people might need access to me, I recognize that this 24-7 situation has had pretty serious effects. The low-lying panic keeps us in a state of hypervigilance, where our fight-or-flight mechanism is working overtime. The exhaustion you feel isn't just from being busy—it's from your brain trying to monitor too many things at once. When you're tracking everyone's location, mood, and needs, you have less mental energy available for the things that are actually your responsibility to do.

Other people's problems become your responsibility and when you don't fix them, you feel inadequate. You don't know how to enjoy good moments because there are terrible things that could happen or they might just disappear.

True relaxation is hard—the world around you doesn't stop because you do.

It's Not Up to You to Keep the World Spinning

So how do we break free from the compulsion to monitor everything? How do we move from unhealthy vigilance to trust? It starts with small, intentional steps that challenge our belief that our attention is what keeps the world spinning.

Practice the phrase "Not my job."

When you catch yourself taking responsibility for outcomes you can't control, remind yourself, *That's not my job.* Your job isn't to prevent your adult daughter from making mistakes. Your job isn't to monitor your husband's stress levels throughout the day. Your job isn't to be the backup plan for everyone else's life. Your job is to be faithful in what God has actually given you to do.

Learning to say "Not my job" requires you to get clear about what *is* your job. Your job is to love people well, not to manage their lives. Your job is to be present for your children, not to prevent them from experiencing any difficulty. Your job is to be a supportive spouse, not to monitor and manage your partner's emotional state throughout the day.

The phrase "Not my job" isn't callous—it brings clarity. When I try to do everyone else's job, I inevitably neglect my own. When you're busy monitoring your teenager's location, you miss opportunities for true connection. When you're managing your friend's crisis, you might be avoiding your own issues. When you're worried about everything that could go wrong, you're not fully present for what's going right.

Distinguish between intuition and vigilance.

Before you check your phone again, ask yourself, *Is this intuition or hypervigilance?*

Intuition whispers; hypervigilance shouts.
Intuition is specific; hypervigilance is vague.
Intuition can wait; hypervigilance can't.
Intuition makes room for love; hypervigilance makes room for control.

Learn to tolerate the withdrawal.

When you start pulling back from constant monitoring, you'll feel uncomfortable—like something important is being left undone. This isn't your intuition telling you to check your phone; it's withdrawal from the addiction to know everything. Sit with the discomfort for five minutes before acting on it. Often the urge will pass, and you'll realize nothing terrible happened while you weren't watching.

Count the cost of constant vigilance.

Most of us have never honestly assessed what our hypervigilance costs us. We focus on what we think it prevents, but we rarely consider what it steals. Make a list of what your constant monitoring has cost you: sleep, presence with your family, peace of mind, trust in relationships, the ability to enjoy good moments.

When you're always scanning for what could go wrong, you can't be fully grateful for the gifts you already have. When you're constantly checking on everyone else, you lose touch with your own needs and desires. When you're living in perpetual "what if" mode, you miss the "what is" right in front of you.

The cost of hypervigilance isn't just your peace of mind—it's your presence, your relationships, your capacity for joy. It's the life you're not living while you're busy monitoring life instead of actually living it.

All these strategies can help break compulsive patterns, but if we're honest, they're about managing our vigilance rather than addressing the deeper issue. We may still be operating from the belief that our attention is what keeps disaster at bay. Even our attempts to be less anxious can become another form of control.

The real question isn't how to be less vigilant—it's whether we can learn to trust that Someone else is watching when we're not. But this kind of trust doesn't come naturally to those of us who learned early that safety depended on our attention. We need to see a different model entirely—Someone who demonstrates what it looks like to rest in the middle of chaos, not because He's irresponsible but because He knows something we don't.

We need to see what it looks like when perfect vigilance

meets perfect peace, when ultimate responsibility is held by Someone who actually has the power to handle it.

The key is to believe that our peace doesn't depend on our monitoring but on the character of the One who never sleeps.

That's a fundamentally different kind of rest than what the world offers. It's not the temporary relief of a vacation or the momentary calm of a meditation app. It's the deep, settled peace that comes from knowing that the most important things are being handled by Someone infinitely more capable than we are.

To understand what this kind of rest looks like, we need to meet Someone who demonstrated it in the most unlikely circumstances—Someone who could sleep through a storm, not because He was checked out but because He knew exactly who was in control.

Don't You Care?

It had been a long day of teaching parables when Jesus decided it was time to hop in the boat and head out. The disciples joined Him, and He told them they were heading to the other side of the lake. We know that this required about eight miles of travel and that this particular body of water was in kind of a tricky spot—known for its intense and unexpected weather.

The Disciples' Story

For more about the disciples and their longing for control, see Mark 4:35-41.

Scripture doesn't tell us how long it took for a storm to rise up, but it does tell us that it was no ordinary shower. In fact, the conditions got so bad that the boat was starting to take on water and death seemed like a legitimate possibility.

Several of the men in the boat were fishermen, and I'm sure they'd been in storms before, so the fact that this one terrified them is saying something. This storm was clearly in a different category, and they panicked while screaming for the Lord.

Meanwhile, Jesus is . . . "Jesus? JESUS!!!!!!"

Well, He was, umm, resting.

As I mentioned, it had been a long day, and parables really take it out of you.

Visualize what's happening here—don't just read it: The boat was starting to take on water and was being thrown around like a rag doll. The hull slapped hard; brine stung the tongue; the deck pitched like a living thing. This seemed like the right time for Jesus to problem-solve, but He slept right through it. Can you imagine how ridiculous it would have been to see a person's body being rattled and soaked while they didn't even wake up?

Scripture tells us that He was asleep on a cushion in the stern of the ship, but a few details add color to the story. He wasn't lying on a giant mattress or lounging somewhere under the deck—He probably had His head on some remedial type of a head cushion and He was right out there in the open with the disciples.

In fact, He was asleep in the stern of the ship, where the

most experienced sailor sat so he could guide the boat and pay attention as they traveled. The One who was supposed to be vigilant to keep them safe had fallen asleep, the oar outside His grasp.

The disciples screamed for Him to wake up, and their question was one that crosses our minds many times in a day: "Don't You care?"

This story is told in three Gospels, each with slight variations from the others. There is one part that's consistent, though, and it's perhaps the most telling detail of all: There is no record of the disciples asking Jesus to calm the water.

The disciples didn't ask Jesus to calm the storm—they asked Him to care. To be present.

This is what we do when we're drowning in vigilance. We don't actually want God to handle the situation—we want Him to be as concerned about it as we are. We want Him to confirm that our worry is appropriate, that our monitoring is necessary, that our vigilance is justified. We want Him to join us in our anxiety rather than invite us into His peace.

But Jesus didn't meet their panic with more panic. He didn't say, "You're right, this is terrible—we should all be worried." Instead, He demonstrated what it looks like to operate from a completely different paradigm, one where ultimate control belongs to Someone who can actually do something about the situation.

At this point in their travels with the Lord, the disciples had never seen Him calm a storm—maybe it never crossed their minds to ask. Only He knew He was capable.

Our job is to ask Him to be with us, not to presume we have the power to know what He will do or how He will intervene.

No matter our vigilance, we cannot control the storm.

The One Who Never Sleeps

I don't think it's a coincidence that this story comes directly after His teaching: In fact, there's one parable in particular that speaks volumes.

Jesus told the crowd what the Kingdom of God is like: "A man scatters seed on the ground. Night and day, whether he sleeps or gets up, the seed sprouts and grows, though he does not know how. All by itself the soil produces grain" (Mark 4:26-28).

One of the most common mistakes an amateur gardener can make is being overzealous in monitoring the seed. They check on it too frequently to see if it is starting to grow, but the tip of the root can be as small as a single cell; it is easily destroyed with interference.

What if our hypervigilance is actually interfering with God's work? What if His true peace comes when we pull our hands out of the soil and marvel at what we can never understand?

After the waters settled that night, Jesus asked the disciples why they were afraid. That's right—at first, they were afraid of the storm. But once Jesus calmed the storm, they were still afraid—but this time they were struck with holy awe. His power could subdue the threat in ways that confirmed that He was the Messiah—it was prophesied in the Old Testament.

They were in awe because they realized He was exactly who He said He was.

Rest, friend. You may not be able to calm the sea, but it answers to God.

I think about that three-year-old girl who couldn't sleep until she checked on everyone, and I realize she was doing the best she could with what she knew. She was trying to love her family the only way she understood how—by staying alert, by monitoring, by making sure everyone was okay. It made sense to her that if she stopped watching, something terrible might happen.

And then, one day, it did.

Not because I turned my back, and not because I failed. One of the hardest and most beautiful things we can ever come to believe is that God is trustworthy even when hearts pound and breath stops.

The truth I've had to learn over and over again is this: My hypervigilance was never what kept anyone safe. My three-year-old checking didn't prevent tragedy from touching my family. My adult monitoring can't control outcomes any more than my childhood anxiety could. The illusion of control that vigilance provides is just that—an illusion.

But here's what I know now that I didn't know then: There's a difference between my watching and His.

When Jesus slept in the stern of that boat, He wasn't being irresponsible. He was demonstrating the rest that comes from knowing who's actually in control. The disciples panicked because they thought safety depended on human vigilance—on staying awake, paying attention, monitoring the situation. Jesus slept because He knew safety depended on divine sovereignty.

He could rest because He trusted His Father, and we can rest for the same reason. This doesn't mean we become careless or checked out. It means we learn the difference between responsible attention and compulsive vigilance. It means we do what's ours to do and trust God with what's His.

In the moments that tempt you to believe He has abandoned His post, soak yourself in this undeniable truth: One way or another, you are safe and sound with the Watchman who never sleeps.

A Benediction for the Weary

You were never meant to hold the world together, and it will not fall apart when you stop trying.

You don't have to brace yourself for every possibility or anticipate every worst-case scenario.

Jesus has taken the night shift—and you can rest, because He never does.

When your heart is tired from carrying what was never yours to carry, may you hear His invitation to peace, not because everything is finished but because He is faithful and His Word is true.

You cannot control every outcome—and that's a gift.

May you loosen your grip when the world feels unsteady, and may you quiet your spirit when life unfolds in ways you never expected.

He will never fail you, beloved. This is true when the waters are calm, and it's true when the horizon is hazy.

The same hands that spun the world into being hold you now, and there's no safer place to stand, even when the storm rages around you.

You can rest. You are held. You are safe.

Amen.

7

When the Ground Beneath You Shifts

You are safe.

The secret of change is to focus all of your energy not on fighting the old but on building the new.

DAN MILLMAN, *WAY OF THE PEACEFUL WARRIOR*

It's 3 a.m. and I'm considering the fact that I don't have as many years ahead of me as I have behind me. I can feel panic rising up as I sweat through my sheets. I want to go back in time and I can't.

I'm at a strange and emotional place in my life right now. I have two daughters who just graduated from college, one who just finished her freshman year in college, and one who will be a freshman in high school next year. This means that I no longer have kids who rely on me the way they did when they were tiny, and truth be told, it's a lot harder than I ever imagined it would be. I know we should celebrate each stage of life, and there is a lot of good these days, but there is a strange emptiness in realizing I will never bring my littles to the pool again, I'll never celebrate their first double-digit birthdays—and I can hardly walk by the baby aisles at Target without getting teary. I have a physical reaction when I see pictures of them in their tiny bathing suits and hair bows.

I can't go back.

I can never go back.

I don't know if other people struggle with this, or to this extent. Every day I reminisce about good ol' days, whether they're from my childhood, early marriage, or days as a mom with young kids, etc. If I spend more than a split second thinking about what the world was like when my dad was still in it, I burst into tears. It is inconceivable that he will never show up at my house in his fedora and Tommy Bahama tropical shirt. I remember the way he tossed his legs over the leather chair in the family room, the way he lit up whenever he saw me, and the endless hours he spent taking care of me and delighting in my kids.

I would do anything in the world to go back, and I can't.

Instead of feeling nostalgic in ways that bring me joy, I struggle with the ache of what has passed me by and wonder if my best days are behind me. I know how the devil works, and this is an area he knows will affect me. There's something disconcerting about the present—we are frozen between the days we left and the days we have left.

I don't like change.

Some people do, but they are freaks.

Actually, I really envy those folks and marvel at their easy-breezy way of facing new adventures.

They get excited about moving to another state for a job opportunity and love when their routine is disrupted. Detours are welcome. A planned day gone awry is no big deal.

I watch these people with genuine fascination and a little bit of resentment. How do they not feel that pit in their stomach when everything familiar disappears? How do they sleep the first night in a new house without lying awake cataloguing everything that's different about the sounds? When they leave a job, are they truly excited about new possibilities, or are they secretly terrified like the rest of us but just better at pretending?

I am such a creature of habit and I operate best when things stay at status quo. The thing is, though, nothing stays the same. We all know it, but we don't necessarily know what to do with it.

Listen, most of us are wired for predictability and steadiness. That's our safe zone—the place where we just keep trucking along and everything around us moves at our pace. Reality has taught us that this isn't how it works, but that doesn't mean we know how to face change in a healthy way when it comes knocking.

A Series of Little Deaths

Here's what's really happening when we resist change: We're putting our security in things that shift instead of in a God who never changes.

There's nothing wrong with appreciating stability and predictability—it's only an issue when we've made it our god. We start to believe that peace comes from our circumstances, so we are rattled when those shift.

I'm not just talking about staying in the same house or keeping the same job; this applies to the versions of ourselves that exist within a time period too. Your identities change just like everything else.

Maybe you were "the mom with little kids," and now you're "the mom with teenagers." Maybe you were "the woman with the career," and now you're "the woman starting over." Maybe you were "the person who had it all figured out," and now you're "the person who has no idea what's next."

It's great to welcome your new roles, but it's also more than okay to grieve the ones that no longer exist. Truth be told, change involves a series of little deaths (I didn't use this as a title because I felt sure it would not fly off the bookshelves). It's true, though. And it's human nature to be resistant when we meet up with the new version of ourselves. We want what's familiar and comfy, even if it doesn't serve us well anymore.

These little deaths are so much more profound than we give them credit for. There's the death of being the person everyone comes to with their problems when your kids become adults who handle things themselves. There's the death of being seen as young and full of potential when people start asking you about retirement plans. There's the death of believing you have unlimited time to become whoever you want to be when you realize some doors really have closed.

There's also the death of certain dreams—not just big ones like career ambitions, but small ones too. The death of family vacations and traditions that don't work now that everyone has different schedules. The death of the version of your marriage that existed when you were united in the trenches of parenting small children. The death of your physical self that could stay up all night or eat whatever you wanted without consequence.

We don't talk about these deaths enough, but they're real, and they accumulate. Each one requires its own form of grief, but we're taught to just "embrace the next season" without acknowledging what we're leaving behind. That's not healthy, and it's not human. These deaths deserve to be mourned before we can fully step into whatever comes next.

Some of the most difficult seasons of change you will ever experience come from not knowing how to let go of who you have been. Sometimes people stay in awful situations because at least they're a familiar kind of awful. The change can feel scarier than settling.

Most of my friends are around my age, and we are all facing similar changes. A few have become empty nesters recently, and it has been fascinating to see how they've dealt with it differently. One of them told me she was living her best life, and another couldn't stop crying because she has no idea who she is outside of being a mother. She dedicated her life to packing lunches and carpooling, and now she feels untethered and without purpose.

The more we find our identity in the roles we play in the world, the less we will know our true identity in Christ.

Easier said than done, eh?

The Space Between

I know what it is like to white-knuckle my way through change and fight the current of time. It is, in a word, unpleasant.

The other day my daughter asked me why I creaked so much, and I disowned her. It's the early empty-nesting strategy that's sweeping the nation.

I hate that we have to acknowledge the things we never got to do or be in our lives, but it's a healthy practice. You're probably not going to go to law school if you're eighty, and if you've never been a swimmer, I don't think you'll be in the Olympics. You might be at a point where you realize you aren't going to be a mother the way you always thought you would be or that you didn't raise the kind of kid you thought you were going to.

I know it's denial, but I am still fully convinced I could throw a cheerleading stunt like I did in college. I maintain this delusion by refusing to attempt it.

Every time change happens, I have to ask myself if I trust God to be in control of it. Am I safe?

What if God and I have different working definitions of safety? Plot twist: We do. My version is keeping myself safe, and His is, well, not that. But what happens if my hands come off the wheel over here? He might give me that job He thinks is best for me but I can already tell it's terrible.

He might tell me to move because He doesn't know I would be happier here. It's best for me to keep Him in line—He's taking care of a lot of people and He might miss something.

I like to inform God that I will change when I'm ready, and He loves to remind me that my track record begs to differ.

Funnily enough, the hard part of change isn't actually the change itself, it's the space that exists between what was and what will be. It's what psychologists call liminal space. The word *liminal* comes from the Latin root meaning "threshold," and it identifies the space between death and resurrection, between where the old identity has died and where the new one will be born. You know what's behind you, but you can't yet see what's ahead. It's the days between the cross and the resurrection—the middle place of uncertainty.

It feels awful there sometimes, and that's okay.

Hear me say this: Just because it doesn't feel like God is in control doesn't change the fact that He is. Your ability to feel something has no bearing on what is true—and that's a relief when you've convinced yourself the sky is falling.

When You Come Face-to-Face with Change

When change comes knocking, how do we practice remembering that God will hold us steady?

Identify your security anchors.

When change feels overwhelming, I'm usually not afraid of the change itself—I'm afraid of losing the things that make me feel secure. That panic when my role shifts isn't really about the new responsibilities; it's my nervous system screaming that if my familiar identity disappears, I won't know who I am anymore. The moment I feel that familiar resistance to change, I try to stop and name what I'm really clinging to. Instead of saying, "Money is tight," I say, "I'm afraid that if we can't maintain our lifestyle, I'll lose the sense that we're 'doing well' and people will see us differently. I'm asking financial status to give me security and respectability that only God's provision can." Then I ask the deeper question: "What am I asking this circumstance to do that only God can do?" This shifts my attention from what I might lose to where my security truly comes from.

Grieve what you should.

Every change requires me to let something die, and I'm terrible at letting go of even the versions of myself that aren't serving me well anymore. When I'm transitioning out of a season, I want to skip the grief and jump straight to the new thing, but that's not how transformation works. Instead, I need to ask the Lord to show me what needs to die so new life can begin, and then I ask for the strength to face it. There are many things I would resurrect that should stay buried, and by asking the Lord to join me in the process, I am drawing a line in the sand about what I'm leaving behind.

Reframe the liminal space.

The hardest part of change isn't the ending or the beginning—it's the middle space, where nothing is clear. That in-between time, when I'm no longer who I was but not yet who I'm becoming, feels like purgatory, and my instinct is to rush through it as fast as possible. But I've learned to see this threshold space differently. Instead of viewing it as empty waiting time, I try to ask God, "What are You teaching me about trust that I can only learn in the uncertainty?" The liminal space isn't punishment—it's where faith is built. I can't see what's ahead, but I can practice believing that God is preparing something good even when I have no evidence of it yet.

Acknowledge small remembrances.

We have daily opportunities to pause and take stock of what's happening around us, noting the faithfulness of God. Even the most insignificant aspects of your life speak to God's providence. The key is to train your mind and heart to be attuned to them. Your kitchen counter tells the story of God's faithfulness through seasons—the coffee mug that was a wedding gift, the school permission slip that needs signing, the reading glasses you never thought you'd need. Everything you are surrounded by speaks to change and God's care through it all. Once we've learned to make trust our default, the bigger shifts don't hold the same fear they used to.

These practices build spiritual muscle memory for the moments when change isn't optional and life shifts unexpectedly.

It's important to be mindful of change so you can move forward without minimizing what has passed. Make markers to signify a new stage, whether it's a journal entry, a conversation, or you know . . . a rock.

The Lord Goes Before You

One of the funny things about remembering the past when we're going through change is that we aren't great at remembering it accurately.

This may be the reason an entire generation of Israelites who had finally escaped slavery complained about the food they missed in Egypt. Hilariously, one of the things they kept talking about was leeks. *Leeks*. Who cares about being enslaved if you've got those suckers, right? So weird.

The Israelite Pilgrims' Story

For more about the Israelites and the way they coped with change, see Joshua 3–4.

But here's what makes their story so relevant to us: It wasn't just the Israelites who originally left Egypt who struggled to trust God through change. So did the next generation—the children who had grown up watching their parents fail the ultimate test of trusting God when things felt out of their grasp. Forty years earlier, their parents had stood at the edge of the Promised Land, seen the giants, and said, "We can't do this. God won't come through." They died in the wilderness because they couldn't trust God with outcomes they couldn't control.

Now it was this generation's turn to face the same terror their parents couldn't survive. They'd inherited more than just their parents' DNA—they'd inherited the fear that trusting

God with major change leads to disappointment. Their entire lives had been shaped by the story that ended with "and then they all died in the desert because they took a risk."

This pattern of inherited fear around change is so much more common than we realize. I see it in my own family—the subtle ways anxiety about change gets passed down unintentionally through generations.

These wounds are tricky because they feel like wisdom or protection, but they can be fear masquerading as discernment; they keep us trapped in familiar dysfunction instead of trusting God with the unknown. The hardest part is that the people who passed these wounds to us usually did it out of love—they were trying to protect us from the pain they experienced. Unfortunately, protection from all risk is also protection from all growth.

Breaking these inherited patterns requires us to examine not just our own fear of change but the stories our families have told us about what happens when people take risks, trust God with uncertainty, or step into new seasons. Sometimes our resistance to change isn't even ours—it's a hand-me-down fear that doesn't fit our situation at all.

The Israelites had been wandering for forty years, and Zillow had some great options. A couple of spies sneaked in and decided it was go-time. This was, in no small part, due to the faith of a prostitute who took a chance on believing God. I wish I had more time here to talk about Rahab, because she's an Old Testament superstar.

Anyway, we pick up the story as they're headed to the land God had promised them. Their resolve had been strengthened, and they had made peace with the leek-less life.

It starts, as all good stories do, by leaving the town of Shittim behind.

That's actually the name, in case you thought I was trying to say something else. What's wrong with you?

Joshua was the leader, and he told all the Israelites they were going to camp out before they crossed the Jordan River. Let me make a quick note here: A megaphone would not have been sufficient for this announcement; there were likely around two million people who were trucking along at this point.

They played a game of extreme telephone, and the word went out: "Consecrate yourselves today, because tomorrow we are stepping into the water that will lead to freedom."

Consecrate yourselves. Something holy is about to happen.

What does it mean to consecrate yourself when you're terrified of the change God is calling you into? Well, in this context it meant that they were to wash their clothes, abstain from sex, and remember that they were set aside by God. But more than external rituals, this was about examining what they really believed about God's character before stepping into life-altering change. For a generation that had only heard stories about what happens when people trust God with change, this consecration was really about excavating their deepest fear: *What if trusting God with this transition ends the same way it did for our parents?*

This is exactly the spiritual discipline we need when change terrifies us: to stop and examine what we really believe about God's character before we're forced to step into transitions we can't control.

In practical terms, this kind of consecration might look like setting aside time to examine the stories we tell ourselves about God when change threatens our security. Do I really believe God is good when I can't see the outcome? Do I trust that His plans for me are better than my plans for me, or do I just say that because it sounds like the right answer?

This consecration process forces me to get honest about the gap between my stated theology and my lived theology. I say I believe God is faithful, but my anxiety about change reveals that I'm not sure He's faithful to me. I say I believe His ways are higher than my ways, but my resistance to change shows that I think my version of safety is better than His version of growth.

The consecration isn't about performing religious activities to earn God's favor before a transition—it's about getting aligned with reality. It's about examining our deepest fears and false beliefs about God's character so we can step into change from a place of truth instead of inherited anxiety. Sometimes this means admitting that I don't actually trust God as much as I thought I did. Sometimes it means acknowledging that my fear of change is really fear that God doesn't have my best interests at heart.

I imagine that the Israelites, who were about to have to live out their faith, were a smidge nervous. Joshua filled them in on some logistics: The ark of the covenant—the physical structure that represented the presence of God—would lead the way. The people were told to stay about a half mile behind it so everyone could see it up ahead. The priests were in charge of carrying it, and Joshua gave them specific instructions: "You guys head out in front of the people, and then they'll all follow you."

A couple of million people, the physical presence of the holy God, and a river we've got to cross.

No way that could go wrong.

The Lord spoke to Joshua, telling him it was time to get going because today was the day He would show the people that He was with them in the same way He was with the last generation at the Red Sea. And it wasn't going to be easy—this was flood season and the water was dangerously high and moving rapidly.

But the Lord was going before them.

The Lord is going before you.

But here's the catch: The water wasn't going to stop raging until the priests put their feet in it. They had to trust the directions the Lord had given them before they could see the miracle He promised. This was trusting God with outcomes you can't control on the ultimate scale—they had to step into life-altering change while everything was still uncertain.

Remember: All the people from the former generation had died, so none of these folks got to see the parting of the Red Sea. They had only known the dusty roads and the stories that had been passed down, but they were about to experience God's faithfulness for themselves. They had never even had a place to call home—they were nomads carrying the inherited wound that said, "Trusting God with change leads to disappointment."

The time had come. The priests dipped their toes in the water and immediately it ceased, leaving a dry road for them to cross. All the while, the priests had to hold up the ark of the covenant. Hopefully they took shifts, because it took four people to hold it on their shoulders, and playing crossing guard for millions of people could not have been an easy task.

Do you see what just happened here? This generation did what their parents couldn't do—they stepped into the unknown while the outcome was still uncertain. Their parents stood at the edge of the Promised Land, saw the giants, and said, "We can't do this. God won't come through." But this generation looked at the flooding Jordan River and said, "We're going in anyway."

The difference wasn't that they were braver or stronger—it's that they had learned to trust God's character more than their ability to control outcomes.

There they were, up against one of the last great battles before they entered the place God had set aside for them. The wanderers were going home.

In the Middle of the Miracle

As the ark was held high, hundreds of thousands of people walked through a miracle while their feet left marks on dry ground. When the last of the group finally made it to the other side, the Lord told Joshua to have one man from each tribe take a rock from the place where the priests had stood with the ark of the covenant and bring it to the place they would camp that night.

Pay attention to what's happening: They were moving the rocks in the middle of the miracle.

There, in the liminal space, they were reminding themselves and the world that God had brought them this far.

The ground was still dry when they took the time to acknowledge the faithfulness of the Lord, but they had no idea what was about to happen. The entire generation before them had been wiped out trying to enter, so I don't think they thought they were home free when they got to this point.

No matter what's happening in your life right now, there is dry ground to be marked. There are places where God has proven trustworthy during transitions when you were terrified He wouldn't be. This isn't just so we can look back and wish we could be there again; it's so we have the courage to face whatever changes come next, even when they're unknown.

God is clear about the reasoning behind placing these rocks: It's so the Israelites could tell their children that the waters of the Jordan stopped when they crossed over—the rocks would serve as a memorial in honor of God for years to come. It was a physical, tangible way to tell those who would come after them that they were standing on holy ground.

But here's what I love most about this story: There were actually two sets of memorial stones. The twelve rocks the men carried to shore were the public testimony, the stones everyone could see and point to when they told the story of God's faithfulness. But Joshua also placed twelve stones right where the priests had been standing with the ark—stones that would be completely hidden once the water rushed back over them.

Some scholars suggest this wasn't an accident. The visible stones were for sharing God's faithfulness with others. The hidden stones were for the intimate, personal reminders between God and His people—the private markers of His faithfulness that only He and they would know about. Sometimes there are markers you share with others to bear testimony to God's work in your life, and there are others that are sacred because they are an intimate part of your relationship with Him.

This distinction between public and private markers of God's faithfulness is so important, especially when we're going through major life changes. The public stones are the testimonies we share—the ways we can point to God's provision, protection, or guidance that others can see and celebrate with us. This might be the job that came through just when we needed it, the relationship that was restored, the healing that happened, the doors that opened when we took a leap of faith.

But the hidden stones are equally important, maybe more so. These are the intimate moments between you and God that no one else witnessed—the peace that flooded your heart in the middle of a sleepless night when you were terrified about the future, the way a specific verse seemed to leap off the page exactly when you needed to hear it, the sudden assurance that everything would be okay even when circumstances looked impossible.

Sometimes the hidden stones are about what didn't happen—the accident you avoided, the temptation you resisted, the harsh words you didn't speak, the action you didn't take that would have been devastating. These invisible protections and moments of guidance are just as much evidence of God's faithfulness as the dramatic, public victories.

I think we need both kinds of memorial stones. The public ones build faith in our communities and give us opportunities to testify to God's goodness, and the hidden ones sustain us in the private moments, when doubt creeps in and we wonder if God really sees us.

From the time the Israelites got to the edge of the Jordan River, they could see the Promised Land, but they had no idea what it would be like to be settled somewhere. They had never been anything but nomads, and the future was uncertain—not just their safety, but what their lives would look like once they got there. What if this change was too much? What if they weren't ready? What if God's plan for their new settled life didn't match what they hoped for?

I'm certain they recalled the sacred ground their feet had walked across, marked by stones, while they were in between what was behind and what was yet to come.

In a very real sense, our lives exist in this same liminal space; we breathe the air of this world while we navigate constant change. Living between the already and the not yet means learning to see what others can't and walking in faith because of the view we have.

Years ago, I was at the beach with my family when darkness swallowed the clear sky and a downpour forced a chaotic rush, as toys were shoved into backpacks and towels turned into makeshift covers. Dozens of families packed up and fled, but a few of us sat still while the rain pounded our beach umbrellas.

I realize how ridiculous we looked, and to a watching world it must have seemed odd. We were sitting there in the relentless, pelting rain, and all the while we waited.

I guess we saw something they didn't: a seam in the sky.

It went from bruised to blue, reminding us that this squall wasn't forever.

I think that's often what the Christian life looks like when you've learned to trust God with change you can't control: sitting in the storm because you've excavated the evidence that God's character doesn't change when everything else does, even if it makes you look absurd to the rest of the world.

We live in the liminal space, daily marking the ways He made Himself known. There is a threshold ahead that will make all things new and right. Until then, we learn to embrace even what we didn't anticipate because it is another opportunity to see His faithfulness.

We will make it to the Promised Land, and God willing,

there will be leeks. Until then, welcome the twists in the road because they always lead to Him.

Blessed be those who believe it while they travel.

A Benediction for Those in Times of Change

When you find yourself between what was and what will be, remember that the Lord is neither surprised nor alarmed. He has seen the pages that will be revealed to you in the coming days. May He turn your fear into curiosity and ease your need for control.

May you look back often to see the markers of His faithfulness and use them as anchors when the world feels unpredictable and dangerous. He is already where you are going, and He has marked out the path that will lead you there. Be of great courage, friend.

8

Made for Connection

You are seen.

Friendship . . . is born at the moment when one man says to another "What! You too? I thought that no one but myself. . ."

C. S. LEWIS

The loneliest part of friendship isn't the absence of people—it's the absence of being seen.

Several years ago, I was in a friendship that, for a season, was marked by trust and deep connection. But over time, something shifted and I could feel the distance between us. There was no dramatic showdown—just a gradual moving away that plainly told me she didn't want to be my friend anymore. There was never a clash or even an argument, just an unexplained distancing that resulted in "How are you?" in a crowd by the pool instead of "How are you?" while I was crumpled on her couch trying to breathe as I reeled with grief. I set aside every piece of pride I had to try to understand it, but I never got any closer to knowing the answer.

It feels as confusing today as it was then, though it doesn't dominate my days anymore. Back then, I cried every week; now I mostly carry it as a quiet ache. The hardest part is not having answers. I asked her over and over, desperate to understand what I had done wrong, but she always responded, "You haven't done anything." That should have been comforting, but it only made the rejection feel more mysterious—and more personal.

What hurt most wasn't the loss—it was the haunting sense that maybe the real me had been exposed and found lacking. If I had known what role I was supposed to play, I would have tried harder to get it right. But there was no script to follow, and that made me feel powerless.

I felt like an idiot—I know I hadn't imagined our friendship. It had been years of closeness and life-sharing. Somehow it became a confusing, difficult loss that left me blindsided and broken.

I've never put this story on paper, and it's harder to tell than I thought it would be—partly because it makes me gun-shy to open myself up again.

Here's something about me that is truly painful: I don't have any lifers. No childhood best friend who was in my wedding, no family full of cousins around the table, no neighbor who knew me since braces and perms. I have plenty of people in my life, but not the kind of rooted friendships that anchor you with decades of shared history. Most days I'm fine with it—until someone else casually mentions their built-in community, and I feel that strange, hollow ache that whispers, "Something's missing."

That's when pretending creeps in—not pretending that I don't care, but pretending that I'm fine without this kind of friendship. Pretending that the ache doesn't exist feels easier than admitting how deep it runs.

There's a grief that comes with recognizing you don't have those foundational relationships that seem to anchor other people. There's no one who can say, "Remember when you were afraid of everything?" or "I always knew you'd end up doing something with words." No shared history of sleepovers and secret-telling, no inside jokes that go back decades, no one who loves you partly because they've watched you grow up.

Also, it's weird to make friends as an adult sometimes. It can feel like it's too late, or it can just seem like an awkward dance. How do I jump in? It's weird as an almost fifty-year-old to say I feel like I'm back in junior high and I don't know who to sit with at the lunch table. And where do you go to start the process? It's genuinely harder to make friends as an adult than it was when we were kids, and it's not just because we're pickier now or more set in our ways. The logistics alone are brutal—between work schedules, family responsibilities, and basic life maintenance, finding time to build new relationships feels nearly impossible.

There's also the vulnerability factor. As adults, we've all been hurt before. We've learned to protect ourselves, to keep our guards up, to be careful about who we let close. We have more to lose now—our reputations, our family peace, our limited emotional energy. The stakes feel higher because we're not just risking our own feelings anymore; we're considering how new relationships might affect our spouses, our children, our carefully constructed routines.

So instead of risking rejection, we perfect our small talk, keep things light, and play it safe. It looks like friendship, but it often feels more like networking. We're showing the edited versions of ourselves, hoping they'll be good enough to get us in the door.

Adult friendships also lack the organic nature of childhood friendships. You can't just show up to someone's house and ask if they want to play. You can't pass notes in class or bond over hating the same teacher. The spaces where adults naturally meet—work, school pickup, neighborhood events—often promote surface-level interactions. How do you transition from "Nice to see you at soccer practice" to "Want to grab coffee and talk about real life?" It feels awkward and forced in a way that childhood friendship never did.

One of the things I'm trying to give myself permission to feel is that being known isn't a black-or-white issue. It isn't like you finally have a conversation and poof—you've done it! It's a process that only you can walk through, and it doesn't have to look like anyone else's. The reality is that I am never going to have childhood friends who knew me in my formative years and have enough history with me to be able to speak into all the ways I have grown and become who I am today.

It's okay to say that this hurts, but it doesn't mean things can't be different now and it doesn't mean it's a bad thing to have my own friendship journey.

Naming the grief is part of moving past the pretending. I don't have to minimize it or explain it away; I can simply admit that it matters—and then open myself to the possibility that God can still give me friendships that look different but are no less real.

If you hear me say one thing in this chapter, I hope it is this: You cannot compare your deep friendships to other people's deep friendships. They all look different, and that's okay. Your perception of what deep means is probably different from theirs, and your needs and desires are individual to you.

Here's a wild thought: Not everyone even wants deep friendships. Some people are perfectly content to skim the surface and flit from party to party without feeling a sense of emptiness. That's okay too. You have to recognize that there are friends who will just want to talk about surface-level topics, and you don't have to go beneath that with everyone; it's okay to not know the life wounds of everyone in your orbit. In fact, it's healthy.

We don't necessarily need lots of people to go deep with. At the end of the day, we long to know we have a few key people who would go to bat for us, who know the real us, and it can be lonely when we don't. I can fill my calendar, surround myself with good company, and still feel that hollow ache if I'm not bringing my whole self. Pretending may keep me in the room, but it will never make me feel at home there.

The Anatomy of a Friendship

Real friendship doesn't happen by accident—it develops through a predictable pattern most people never notice. There's a reason some people seem to effortlessly build deep connections while others stay stuck in small talk for years. It's not personality or luck—it's understanding how friendship actually works.

The difference between acquaintances and close friends isn't just time spent together; it's the type of interactions you have during that time. You can know someone for years and still be strangers if you never move past surface-level exchanges. But you can also develop genuine closeness with someone relatively quickly if you understand the progression of friendship building.

Here's what most people get wrong about adult friendship: They assume it should feel as effortless as it did when they were kids. But childhood friendship is built on proximity and shared activities—you become friends with whoever sits next to you in class or lives down the street. Adult friendship requires intentionality, because now we have more choices, more competing priorities, and frankly, higher standards.

And when intentionality feels scary, many of us default to pretending—polished small talk, the version of ourselves that feels least risky. It keeps us safe, but it also keeps us shallow.

The good news is that adult friendships can be deeper and more satisfying than childhood ones because they're chosen rather than circumstantial. When someone chooses to invest in a friendship with you as an adult—with all their options and obligations—that means something different than playground proximity.

What creates lasting friendship versus temporary connection? Psychologists have identified several key factors: mutual vulnerability, shared experiences (especially challenges worked through together), consistent availability, and what researchers call responsiveness—the feeling that someone really sees you and cares about your well-being.

The magic ingredient most people miss is reciprocal investment. Friendship isn't about finding someone who meets all your needs—it's about finding someone who's willing to invest in building something meaningful together. You both have to be willing to show up, be vulnerable, and prioritize the relationship even when it's inconvenient. Performing might get you liked, but only reciprocity gets you loved.

Research has shown that the number of hours you spend with people affects your closeness to them. One study found that people need about two hundred hours together in order to feel that they are close friends.[1] But it's not just about logging time; it's about accumulating enough shared experiences that you develop patterns of trust, inside jokes, mutual understanding, and emotional safety. Here's the catch: Those hours don't count if you're faking it. A hundred coffee dates of pretending won't add up to one hour of being real.

The journey from stranger to close friend typically follows a predictable path, though the timeline varies. Understanding these stages can help you recognize where you are with different people and what's needed to move deeper.

- **Surface-level interaction:** You're friendly, maybe you exchange pleasantries at school pickup or chat briefly at church, but the conversation stays safe. You know basic facts—where they work, how many kids they have—but nothing that would surprise anyone else who knows them casually. There's no real investment yet, just politeness and social lubrication.
- **Casual friendship:** You've found some common ground and genuinely enjoy each other's company. You might grab coffee occasionally or linger to chat. You know some personal details—maybe they've mentioned that their husband travels a lot for work or that their teenager is going through a rough patch. You're still presenting your "best self" most of the time, sharing victories more readily than struggles.
- **Developing friendship:** You start to see each other's quirks and imperfections, and instead of being turned off, you find them endearing—or at least acceptable. You begin to confide smaller worries or frustrations, real enough to test the waters. You make plans instead of just running into each other. You might share something slightly embarrassing and find they respond with understanding rather than judgment.
- **Close friendship:** This is where you've seen each other under pressure—through stress, disappointment,

or conflict—and still choose to invest. You know each other's patterns. You can be honest about difficult topics. You've built enough trust that misunderstandings don't unravel the relationship. At least once, you've weathered something hard together and come out stronger.

The key is recognizing that you can't skip stages or force the timeline. Each level requires different kinds of risk. Trying to leapfrog from casual to close almost always backfires.

Of course, not all friendships are healthy ones. Some patterns drain us instead of helping us grow.

- **The Chronic Complainer:** This person always has drama but never wants solutions.
- **The One-Upper:** This person can't let you have a moment—they always need the last word.
- **The Gossip:** This person bonds through other people's secrets but can't be trusted with yours.
- **The Fair-Weather Friend:** This person is fun in the good times but disappears in the hard ones.
- **The Boundary Pusher:** This person ignores your no and makes you feel guilty for having limits.

Trust your gut. If someone consistently leaves you drained, criticized, or like you have to perform to keep their interest, that's not friendship—it's a transaction.

How to Make a Friend

Listen, it's better to have a few close friends than a million acquaintances. But it takes work to move someone from acquaintance to friend.

So where do you start?

Start with inventory, not addition.

You don't have to run out and make five new friends tomorrow. A good place to begin is by looking at the people already in your life. Pay attention to what you offer one another. Some friends make you laugh until you cry. Others are steady encouragers who will pick up the phone no matter what. Others might be deep thinkers who challenge you and stretch you. And then there are the ones who, if you're honest, leave you feeling a little smaller every time you walk away. Taking inventory isn't about ranking people like a popularity contest—it's about being honest about what's growing in the relational soil you're planted in. If you only pour energy into shallow soil, you can't be surprised when the roots don't hold.

Look for the bright lights and follow them.

If you long for more meaningful connection, you have to make some effort to move toward it. Sometimes the people who become the brightest lights in your life don't look anything like what you expected. They might not be your age or share your exact interests or dress like you. They might push you out of your comfort zone—but in ways that feel strangely safe. Pay attention to the ones who leave you feeling more alive, more like yourself, and more like the person God is shaping you to be. Those are usually clues worth following.

Put yourself in repeated-exposure situations.

Strangers don't typically knock on your door and ask if they can hear about your deepest wounds. (They do show up to sell you a new roof after a hailstorm, but that's not the same thing.) Real friendship takes overlap—spaces where you see the same people again and again without the pressure of becoming instant best friends. Serving on a team, joining a group, volunteering in the same place—these are the ordinary environments where trust can grow slowly. Familiarity breeds safety, and safety makes room for depth.

Give the gift of going first.

This one is hard. It means you tell more than the highlight reel. You let someone see beyond the polished details you'd share with a stranger. Not all at once—not a trauma dump on the second coffee date—but small, real pieces of who you are. Mention that you're nervous about your teenager learning to drive. Admit that you felt discouraged at work. Share a story about parenting that wasn't your best moment. These aren't deep confessions, but they're enough to test whether someone can hold your vulnerability with care. Vulnerability is a seed. When you plant it carefully and wisely, it has a chance to grow into trust.

Here's the tricky part: Timing and dosage matter. Share too much too fast, and you'll overwhelm someone. Share too little for too long, and you'll never get past pleasantries. Real friendship requires discernment—and the courage to keep offering pieces of yourself even when it feels risky.

Because here's the truth: The only way to find out if someone can love the real you is to give them the chance to meet the real you. Pretending might feel safer, but it guarantees loneliness. Authenticity feels scarier, but it's the only way to belong.

This slow, ordinary accumulation of trust is exactly how Jesus built His closest relationships. And believe me—they were a ragtag bunch who never would have passed a compatibility test. Yet over shared meals, long walks, laughter, conflict, and grace, they became family.

The Ingredients for Community

When we think about a solid team in the Bible, it's hard to find any group more tight knit than the guys who traveled with Jesus during His three-year ministry.

One day He was cruising along the shoreline and saw Simon (Peter) and Andrew, and He told the brothers to follow Him. He didn't say it in a gentle "You can follow Me if you want to" kind of way. The original Greek gives us insight into the tone, which was more of an imperative than an invitation.

The Disciples' Story

For more about Jesus' apostles and the community they formed, see Matthew 10:1-4.

Maybe you picture Him recruiting the disciples like I do: They were in the middle of a task (say, cleaning fish guts off the dock), and He told them to drop everything and leave their lives behind. That was a pretty bold ask from someone they didn't even know, isn't it? Talk about jumping into the deep end of friendship. It wasn't long before they came across James and John in a boat on the same lake, and He called them to come along.

Like, did they pack up? What do you bring for this sort of thing? Layers. I bet it was layers.

I mean, some of them were married—did they just bail on their wives and kids? Some were part of a family business. They owed money to people and had to make sure there was food on the table and a carpool to ballet. The whole situation seems intense. Why would they leave everything behind, all at once?

Well, they didn't.

Let's pull the lens back for a minute so you can visualize what this really looked like. The town of Capernaum, near where Jesus called most of the disciples, was an extremely small place, with a population of about 1,500 people. My high school had around 2,000, so that really puts it in perspective. In fact, Capernaum was only a few acres of land and more like a little fishing village than a town.

Jesus wasn't telling the disciples to walk away from their lives at that point, He was simply telling them to walk with Him through the village. They slept in their beds that night (Jesus didn't have a house, so He was bunking with Peter at his place). No suitcases, no big commitments. Their lives didn't stop as their friendships formed—and neither do ours.

Jesus was creating community the way community actually forms: with ordinary people, in ordinary places, through ordinary daily interactions.

Not long after the first four disciples were called, Jesus brought Matthew into the mix. This was super controversial because he was the one who collected taxes from their fishing business and wasn't exactly on workout-buddy terms. In fact, the other guys despised him.

It's worth noting that while they probably saw him several times a week, they never would have considered being his friend—their lives were in opposition to one another. Until Jesus came around.

This is one of the clearest pictures in Scripture of how true friendship works: not through compatibility, but through calling. These men didn't "click" at first. In fact, they had every reason to perform, to posture, or to keep each other at arm's length. And yet walking with Jesus became the context where masks could fall, where rivalry softened into brotherhood, and where the real work of trust was forged.

They were now a band of brothers living daily life with Jesus while He performed miracles and shook up the Pharisees. It's unlikely that the disciples didn't at least recognize all the people they came in contact with during those early days of ministry, which makes it all the more intimate.

In the years this crew spent together, they saw their worlds turn upside down. They saw miracles, but they also witnessed tragedy. They laughed together, but they certainly grieved as well.

They knew each other's oddities ("Peter, you've got to stop blurting things out and cutting off people's ears.") and weaknesses, but they also knew their strengths and successes.

You don't need to find a perfect group of people who will never disappoint you. You need to find people willing to do the slow work of building trust, working through conflict, and showing up consistently, even when it's inconvenient. You need people who understand that real friendship isn't about avoiding problems—it's about solving them together.

The disciples didn't start as best friends. They started as coworkers who decided to take a chance on something deeper. They built their relationships through ordinary moments, survived conflict through commitment to something bigger than themselves, and created a community strong enough to change the world.

They never could have weathered the dusty trails together without taking the first steps.

It was the constant movement, the side by side, that showed them they were built for the long haul. They had seen one another succeed and fail, but they loved one another in spite of their humanity.

Peter may have been the one who denied Christ three times, but he was also the one who walked on water and called Jesus the Savior of the world.

Thomas doubted, but he also fell at the feet of Jesus.

The extraordinary moments were born from the ordinary ones, and history was made one relationship, one conversation, one hour at a time. Just as it is for each of us.

A Benediction for the Lonely

May the Lord bless you in the small conversations that build trust, and in so doing, give you the courage to let people know you. May you know how deeply the Lord treasures you and longs for you to find relationships that encourage your love for Him.

May the ordinary moments lead you to extraordinary friends. May you find people who see your quirks, laugh at your stories, sit with your grief, and still stay. And may those friendships become the places where pretending dies and your soul can finally rest.

9

A Good Kind of Hurt

You are brave.

If you want peace, you don't talk to your friends. You talk to your enemies.

DESMOND TUTU

Let's play a game of choose your worst nightmare, shall we?

"I'll take 'Angie, I need to talk to you about something' for $1,000, Alex."

Whoever came up with the notion that healthy disagreement exists was clearly on some kind of hippie drugs.

Here's what I learned about conflict growing up: You'll hurt the people around you and the emotional fallout isn't worth it. The better option is to keep it all bottled up until you explode in rage—people love that. If something is wrong, pretend it isn't. Avoid confrontation at all costs because there will never be a scenario where the other side makes your relationship better.

Most of my greatest fears are tied to doing something that might make people dislike me or choose to walk away. If I tell you that I'm angry or point out something you did that I think was wrong, you'll associate that conversation with me for the rest of your life and things will never go back to normal.

You know what really stinks? The few times I have tried to confront someone in a healthy way and faced the lies I grew up believing, the relationships shifted and I don't think we ever fully got our footing back. It became a mark that floats between us, even in the light moments.

I was telling another friend about this a few weeks ago and was really honest about how hard it was and how I wished I hadn't said anything.

Sometimes it seems easier to live with the lie than the fallout of the truth.

This particular friend has done a lot more therapy than I have and she said something I will never forget: "If you ever need to just test it out, I'm here. I'm safe for you to practice with, and I'm not going to leave."

Maybe one day I'll take her up on it, but honestly even the idea feels risky.

I should add that my husband would never tell you that I have a problem with conflict as it relates to the two of us—I can be pretty callous about it and move on quickly because the whole working-through-it thing is sometimes overrated when you've been married more than a few decades.

I am of the mind that not every disagreement needs to be dissected and processed. Sometimes it's just a bad Tuesday and you have a minute you're not proud of and you call it what it is and watch a movie.

If you're wondering why I'm writing this chapter, you are in good company.

The bottom line is that I somehow vacillate between avoidance at all costs and selective bomb-dropping without much in between. Todd is sometimes like a prisoner of war, which in retrospect, would have added some color if we'd added that to our wedding vows.

In all seriousness, though, healthy conflict was not modeled for me. I don't think I'm alone in that, and I have a feeling most people don't have memories of their parents using textbook approaches to disagreement.

In my family, someone got hurt. Not physically, but in a way that left a wound that you would pay for on the back end. The casualties weren't worth the war.

When it comes to conflict, there's so much at stake. Once you've said it, there's no going back. But as risky as it is, the avoidance of conflict is quite possibly one of the greatest obstacles to our ability to live authentic, deeply rooted lives.

The High Cost of Avoiding Conflict

What we don't talk about enough is the toll that constant conflict avoidance takes on our bodies and our souls. When you spend your days monitoring every word, editing every response, and swallowing every frustration, your nervous system never gets to rest. You're constantly in a state of low-grade hypervigilance, scanning for threats to relational harmony and adjusting your behavior accordingly.

The physical symptoms are real: tension headaches from clenching your jaw when you want to speak up, stomach issues from swallowing your words along with your feelings, insomnia from replaying conversations you wish you'd had differently. Your body keeps the score of every conflict you've avoided, every truth you've buried, every time you've chosen false peace over authentic relationship.

Emotionally, the cost is even higher. You start to lose touch with your own voice because you've spent so much time modulating it for other people's comfort. You begin to doubt your own perceptions because you've trained yourself to dismiss your feelings rather than express them. The constant self-editing creates a kind of internal split—there's the person you are in your head, with all your real thoughts and feelings, and there's the person you present to the world, carefully calibrated to avoid any ripples.

Spiritually, conflict avoidance becomes a form of hiding from God too. When we're so afraid of human disapproval that we silence our authentic selves, we're essentially telling God that other people's opinions matter more than His calling on our lives. We start to believe that keeping the peace is more important than speaking the truth in love, that avoiding discomfort is more valuable than growing in Christlike character.

The tragedy is that all this effort to protect our relationships often ends up damaging them anyway. People can sense when you're not being real with them, even if they can't put their finger on what's happening. The very thing we're trying to preserve—authentic connection—gets sacrificed on the altar of artificial harmony.

So what does healthy conflict look like? What is the goal, and why is it worthwhile? How do we learn to come to it as an opportunity instead of a threat?

It starts with understanding that the absence of conflict does not mean the presence of peace. The Lord calls us to be peacemakers, not peacekeepers—and those are radically different.

Peacekeepers bury problems and pretend nothing is wrong. They are motivated by fear—specifically that people will leave or think poorly of them. They avoid conflict because they're afraid that once it starts, it will never end. They think that keeping peace is a virtue, and they stay away from causing what others might perceive as drama. They think that if they keep everyone happy, they'll somehow manage to keep themselves safe. But peacekeeping is exhausting work, and it never actually creates the safety it promises.

Peacemakers, on the other hand, aren't afraid to seek to understand others before they are understood, and they are more curious than defensive. They are willing to be uncomfortable temporarily because they believe their relationships can withstand hard conversations. They are motivated by love—the love of truth and the love of the other person. They are willing to fight for what is good because they believe it will strengthen the relationship and bring a level of intimacy that wasn't there before.

The difference between these two approaches changes everything. One keeps you stuck in the shallows, managing the surface while the deep currents remain untouched. The other invites you into deeper waters, where real connection happens.

Overestimating Future Pain

I can't begin to tell you how many imaginary conversations I've had with myself because I'm too scared to have them in person. The good news is that I'm always right, but the bad news is that, you know, it never happened.

When we have these talks with ourselves, the script starts to take root, and either we feel overly justified or we're convinced it will be the end of our relationship. We can see the other person's face tightening and hear them snap instead of listen. We can't seem to come up with a scenario in our minds where it goes well.

When I shift from the imaginary conversation to thinking about how it would go in real life, my brain mixes up a cocktail of humiliation, anxiety, and regret.

But here's something that might change how you think about conflict forever: You're probably terrible at predicting how it will actually go. Scientists call this *affective forecasting*, which is a fancy way of saying we're really bad at guessing how we'll feel about things in the future.[1]

That conversation you've been avoiding for three weeks? The one that's been playing on repeat in your head while you're trying to fall asleep? You've probably imagined seventeen different ways it could go wrong, calculated the precise facial expression the other person will make when you bring it up, and rehearsed your defensive responses to things they haven't even said yet.

But here's what research shows: We consistently overestimate how bad we'll feel and for how long. We imagine emotional devastation that rarely materializes. We predict relationship-ending disasters from conversations that often end with, "I'm glad we talked about this."

The science behind this is fascinating and infuriating at the same time. Our brains are essentially time-travel machines that consistently lie to us about the future. We take our current emotional state (usually anxiety or frustration) and project it onto the future scenario. If you're already feeling tense about the conversation, your brain assumes that tension will only escalate. We also have something called *focusing illusion*—we zoom in so intensely on the potential negative outcome that we can't see anything else.[2]

We're also terrible at remembering that most people are more reasonable than we give them credit for. When you're imagining their reaction, you're probably envisioning their worst moment rather than their typical response. You're not factoring in their capacity for growth, their love for you, or their own desire for the relationship to work.

The worst part is that the longer you avoid the conversation, the worse your predictions become. Each day of avoidance adds another layer of catastrophic thinking. What started as *This might be uncomfortable* becomes *This will definitely destroy everything*, simply because you've had more time to imagine increasingly dramatic scenarios.

The reality is that most conflicts, when approached with love and humility, end somewhere in the boring middle ground—not with fireworks or devastation, but with increased understanding and maybe even relief that the tension has been addressed.

The thing is, I don't want to rattle the atmosphere. I'd rather believe I can get over it and move on. Forget conflict—I need a three-day training camp to prep for making an appointment with the dentist.

So I avoid it. I keep the conversation between myself and myself. That way I get to express what I need to, but there is no fallout.

You learned the unspoken rule as a child: *This is how we handle things.* Eventually we come to believe that it's more admirable to take it on the chin than admit something that could cause friction. In your home growing up, conflict may have been catastrophic and you've walked through life thinking of it as a loaded gun. Or maybe you learned that civilized women pretend they're oblivious to anything that could cause dissension because it was below them. Make dinner, not discord.

You know what's funny? That people feel so weird about telling you there's something in your teeth. You didn't do anything to cause the spice particle to get stuck, but somehow it's still embarrassing. And we feel awful about causing shame by pointing it out. This whole thing is ridiculous, but it's how it is. We tiptoe around the possibility of hurting someone so much that we missed the opportunity to step in and help.

It's way worse to get home and wonder why no one mentioned the head of lettuce between your front teeth. You might have felt uncomfortable for a moment if they had, but because they didn't, you've been clueless all day.

We aren't keeping peace, we're maintaining distance.

Distance requires careful management, and it's exhausting. Don't say certain things. Adjust your behavior when the temperature shifts. Be guarded but not in ways they can detect. Monitor, monitor, monitor. Ironically, none of these things ever make us feel safer—they just remind us that the relationship is fragile and should be handled accordingly.

Racking Up Conflict Debt

Distance doesn't just provide separation; it allows debt to accumulate. If you miss a payment, you'll be charged interest. If you ignore it, what started as a manageable situation becomes an overwhelming burden.

Every time you bite your tongue when someone interrupts you repeatedly, that's conflict debt.

Every time you smile and nod when someone makes a comment that stings, more debt. Every time you change the subject instead of addressing the elephant in the room, the interest starts compounding.

As debt adds up, it spreads into other parts of the relationship, and suddenly things you never would have noticed become evidence. You start getting hypersensitive around other people too—all of a sudden you're seeing the world through a distorted lens. Every interaction becomes filtered through the lens of unresolved tension.

Meanwhile, your nervous system is keeping track of all this unexpressed anger and hurt. It shows up as tension in your shoulders when you see their name on your phone. It creates that pit in your stomach when a family gathering approaches. Your body is carrying the weight of all the words you never said, all the boundaries you never set, all the times you chose false peace over authentic relationship.

The other person often has no idea any of this is happening—they think everything is fine because you never told them differently. So they keep doing the thing that hurts you, not out of malice but out of ignorance, while you silently accumulate resentment that will eventually have to go somewhere.

Meanwhile, the other person starts to sense something has shifted. They can't put their finger on it, but the air feels different between you. Your responses are shorter. You're sharing less. There's a subtle coolness they don't understand, so they start pulling back too.

Before long, you're both maintaining a polite distance, wondering what happened to the closeness you used to have. The unspoken truth has created a gap that grows wider every time you choose silence over honesty.

The tragedy is that most of these debts start with something small—something that could be resolved with a five-minute conversation. But compound interest is ruthless, whether we're talking about money or relationships.

So all this begs the question: What does healthy conflict look like?

Pauses and realizes she is still holding the microphone.

First of all, it's (unfortunately) not a lack of tension. I hate to say it, but it's true. Surgery is painful, but it's done for a purpose.

The trouble comes when we start caring more about having our say than the state of the relationship.

You know it's bad when you're writing and something you typed out makes you stop dead in your tracks.

No one needs to shout or rage. There is no storming out. There is give-and-take that keeps the rope in the middle of the tug-of-war. No one wins and no one loses.

No one is talking over the other person or making points just to be hurtful. We aren't tucking away responses and waiting to unload them in a moment of silence. We consider what is being said before we launch an attack. There is room for us to say we're hurt without using feelings as weapons—and the more we know people, the more dangerous the threat.

There is an unspoken agreement to protect the dignity of the other person—and enough humility to admit fault. We circle back to make sure things aren't being taken out of context or misunderstood.

Above all else, there is a sincere desire to repair what has been torn apart and a mutual desire to honor what the Lord is doing in the other person's life.

There can be no healthy conflict without the guidance of the Holy Spirit—our flesh is simply too proud to allow it.

We may be able to come up with textbook responses for the sake of checking a box, but without divine intervention, heart change will never come.

You can only do your part, but you can learn to do it well. Eventually you will build a roster of situations that went better than you anticipated and experiences that reestablished a trust you thought was threatened.

Tips for Healthy Conflict

When you're learning how to have the kind of conflict that honors the Lord (and the other person), here are a few things that will help.

Separate what you can and can't control.

When you're in conflict, the temptation is to try to control both the message and the response. But you only get to manage one of those. You can't control how the other person hears it, how they process it, or whether they agree. You can control whether you speak respectfully, whether you listen, and whether you choose to keep engaging instead of shutting down. Make peace with the truth that influence is not the same as control—and that the absence of control is not the absence of safety.

Challenge your what-if thoughts.

Before you enter a difficult conversation, notice how often your mind runs to worst-case scenarios. Instead of asking

"What if this goes badly?" flip it: "What if this actually brings us closer?" "What if they surprise me?" That shift doesn't guarantee the outcome, but it primes your brain to look for moments of connection instead of scanning for threats.

Practice letting go in small ways.

If you're used to scripting everything in your head, try loosening your grip in low-stakes conversations. Let a silence stretch without rushing to fill it. Ask a question you don't already know the answer to. Resist the urge to rephrase your point until it's "perfect." Small acts of release train you to tolerate the unknown in bigger moments.

Name the win before you begin.

Before you start the conversation, decide what a win really looks like. If your only measure is "convince them I'm right," you've already narrowed your chances of success. Sometimes the win is, "We understand each other better" or "We can talk about this without raising our voices." Defining this ahead of time helps you steer the tone and keeps you from escalating over details that don't matter.

Use the "last 10 percent" rule.

We often hold back the most important part—the last 10 percent of what's on our mind—because it feels risky. But that last bit is usually the piece that explains why you care so much. Try sharing it in a way that's clear but kind: "The reason this matters to me is because . . ." or "What I'm afraid of if we don't solve this is . . ."

Switch from "you" to "I" language.

It's simple, but it works. "You never listen" sounds like an accusation; "I feel unheard" opens the door to understanding. You can still express frustration but without forcing the other person to defend themselves before they can hear you.

I think conflict is just one of those things you have to practice (and fail at) before you start to get the hang of it. Ultimately the goal isn't just to fix things with other people; it's to be sanctified and made more like Jesus. Eventually we come to trust the people who are brave with their words and gentle with our hearts because we know the difference between attack and the desire to see us move toward Jesus.

Is it easy? Comfortable? Predictable? No, but I hope you find it is worth the risk.

Speaking the Message God Gives You

The lady was just trying to take a bath on a roof, okay? We've all been there.

Her name was Bathsheba, and King David decided she would be his as soon as he saw her and her loofah. The only reason he even saw her was because he was a coward who had sent an army off to war while staying safe in his palace. One of those men was an honorable guy named Uriah, who happened to be married to the object of David's affection. Have no fear, Dave had a plan to get what he wanted.

First, he did what respectable men do: He sent a message to her, put on some Barry White, and waited for her to come over. (Not that she had much of a choice, seeing as he was, well, the *king*.)

One thing led to a lot of things, and before you know it, she was pregnant. This was going to be hard to explain to her husband, who was, you know . . . not there. First, David tried to get Uriah to sleep with her so the baby would seem to be his, but it didn't work. So he turned to plan B and sent Uriah to the front lines to guarantee he died in war.

It worked, and David swooped in to comfort Bathsheba and care for her while she carried their baby. By all accounts, this was the beginning of a love story the likes of which Hallmark has never seen.

"Small town girl meets king and . . ." Well, the bones are good, but this is going to need a lot to work in production.

David and Nathan's Story

For more about David and Nathan and the way they dealt with conflict, see 2 Samuel 11–12.

Some time passed, and one day David's friend Nathan swung by. Nathan was more than a friend to David—he was a spiritual adviser and trusted companion. He was a prophet of the Lord, and he was there to do some unpleasant business. You see, God had spoken to him, and he knew that David had sinned. Because Nathan loved David so dearly, he knew this matter had to be dealt with directly, and he didn't shy away from the opportunity.

He was wise in the way he confronted David—he told him a parable designed to make it clear that one person had wronged another. When David showed outrage and demanded that the lesser man be vindicated, Nathan explained that David himself was the sinner. He spoke the words the Lord gave him, telling David there will be a steep price to pay for his choices.

Nathan didn't pound on the door and scream at David, and he didn't act with righteous indignation. He was honest, but not hurtful. The true separation was between David and God, which made it worth the difficult conversation.

In healthy confrontation, the goal is always restoration—not just with each other, but with Jesus. The wounds of a friend come from a place of love, not fear.

Nathan didn't want to destroy David—he loved him too much to watch him be destroyed.

In response, David crumbled. He had been living with his sin for months, and I imagine there was some relief in being exposed. David didn't make excuses, and he didn't try to justify his behavior—in fact, he didn't say a word about it. He simply confessed that he had sinned against the Lord.

In my mind's eye, I picture Nathan being more worried about David than angry with him. There's no indication that he shamed or judged him—he spoke exactly the words the Lord had given him.

Nathan told David that he would live, but as a result of his sin, his son would die.

I wonder if Nathan embraced him in helplessness, crying as if this was his grief to bear too.

You might assume that was the end of Nathan's relationship with David. It's one of those conversations that seems like an irreversible dumpster fire for a friendship. Nathan had just prophesied over David in one of the worst moments of his life, and if ever there was a moment for either of them to walk away, this was it.

But they didn't.

Nathan said what he needed to say, and he loved David no differently. David, for his part, didn't slam the door in Nathan's face and stop returning his texts.

This is the way of the gospel.

In the coming days, David would weep and fast while his son grew sicker. Seven days later, he took his last breath. Nathan might not have been there in person at that moment, but I am certain he walked the long road of grief alongside his friend.

In Bathsheba and David's grief, another son was conceived—you know him as Solomon, but that wasn't his only name. When he was born, Nathan sent word to David and blessed him with the name Jedidiah, which means "beloved of God."

David and Nathan's deep friendship continued for all the days of David's life. In fact, David had many sons, one of which he named Nathan.

As David lay on his deathbed, Nathan came to his side to ensure that Solomon would inherit the throne as was prophesied by the Lord. After David was gone, Nathan served Solomon honorably.

They lived their lives as brothers in the Lord—through sin, death, grief, and joy. No doubt their relationship was forged through all these ups and downs.

We can't be afraid of what will happen if we have conflict, because it paves the way for us to be more like Christ.

When a friend speaks words out of love that might hurt me, I pray that I will have a humble enough spirit to hear what they have to say.

A Benediction for Conflict Avoiders

May you remember that peace doesn't mean an absence of tension and conflict doesn't mean the end of a relationship. When anger or frustration surface, may the Holy Spirit settle you and remind you that you aren't alone.

May your words be kind and your boundaries defined, and may you forgive when necessary. May your heart be soft and your mind clear, and may the Lord honor every opportunity for unity.

10

The Tender Places of Your Soul

You are known.

To be loved but not known is comforting but superficial. To be known and not loved is our greatest fear. But to be fully known and truly loved is, well, a lot like being loved by God. It is what we need more than anything. It liberates us from pretense, humbles us out of our self-righteousness, and fortifies us for any difficulty life can throw at us.

TIM KELLER

When I walk into a room, I don't assume people want me there, and when I walk out, I assume people are talking about me. And not in a good way, either.

Man, I'd love to have that kind of confidence, though. *Now that I'm out of earshot, they're probably discussing my amazing dress and sparkling personality. They're probably going over every single thing I said so they can relive my brilliance. I love being me.*

No, my internal monologue is something like, *I talked too much again. I shouldn't have said that. I should probably replay the whole night and analyze it until I vomit and then choose the hermit life.*

Listen, vulnerability can happen just from showing up.

Every day, you put yourself in situations where you're going to be judged and dissected, even if it isn't malicious.

This chapter was the hardest for me to dig up a story for, and it's not because I'm great at being vulnerable—it's because sometimes I feel like my entire life is an act of vulnerability and I don't particularly want to write about it.

I tried to hire a ghostwriter, but I didn't want to tell her enough to inspire her.

The funny thing is that I would consider myself a person who is very comfortable opening up. I will tell you difficult, emotional, embarrassing things even if I don't know you, and nothing is really off the table. In general, I welcome opportunities to open up to others and am rarely uncomfortable doing so.

Let me clarify: I am comfortable sharing things that I am comfortable with sharing.

I will tell you deep, meaningful stories. I will cry because I'm one of those people who doesn't feel like I need to be embarrassed about crying in front of others. I have no shame when it comes to letting people in as long as I'm in charge of what I want to let them into.

For now, just know that there have been very, very few people I have let into the most sacred, private, and broken parts of myself. I, like most other people, fear that if others saw me at my most vulnerable, they would reject me. It's one thing for that to be hypothetical, but it's even harder to be vulnerable after your worst fear has been confirmed and someone does reject you after you've opened up to them.

It's risky business, this vulnerability thing. When you've been truly vulnerable with someone and they walk away, it doesn't just hurt—it rewrites your understanding of what vulnerability costs.

I talked about the loss of a friendship earlier, and I think when you get to the bones of it, it hurt because I thought that if I was genuine, authentic, and loving, people would stick around. I thought that showing up as my real self was a gift I could give to others, and they would treasure it the way I treasured their true self. I didn't realize I was operating under the assumption that vulnerability is a guarantee to deeper connection, not a risk that could potentially end in rejection. When someone you've been real with chooses to leave—not because of a fight or a betrayal, but simply because they don't want to know you anymore—it teaches you something devastating: Your authentic self might not be enough. Or worse, it might be too much.

That's the fear that lives underneath all our careful curating, our surface-level sharing, our reluctance to let people see us without our masks. It's not just the fear that they won't like what they see—it's the terror that they'll see exactly who we are and decide we're not worth staying for.

This is the vulnerability dilemma that every human faces: We desperately want to be known and loved, but we're terrified that being known will cost us love. We want intimacy, but we're afraid of what intimacy requires.

Here's what I've learned, though: It's miserable to feel rejected and misunderstood, but it doesn't change who I am. It makes me feel things I wouldn't wish on another person, but my identity cannot be shaken.

The One who knows me the best loves me the most, and there's nothing that will change that.

Why It's Risky to Let People In

If vulnerability only meant letting people see behind the mask, anyone could do it. The problem isn't what we choose to do; it's what we feel based on how the other person responds.

The truth is, we believe if we let people see the real us—the mess, the struggle, the imperfections—they'll reject us and we'll be alone. This fear runs deep because it touches our deepest needs: to be known and loved.

We want to be known, but we're terrified of what people will do with that knowledge.

So we shape ourselves into palatable versions—ones that fit the mood, meet expectations, and never make anyone uncomfortable. But concealing our true selves doesn't actually protect us from rejection. It reinforces the belief that our false selves are the only ones people will love. It's profoundly lonely and exhausting to be surrounded by people who know a version of you that requires constant maintenance.

It's one more way we look to the world to tell us who we are.

Charles Cooley called it the "looking-glass self"—the idea that we come to see ourselves as we imagine other people see us.[1] If you were constantly told you were too much when you were young, you learned to conceal those parts of yourself because they were linked to shame. And it makes sense—when we're kids, we have needs (being loved, fed, protected), and those needs feel like they're at risk if we displease the people in charge.

When I was younger, people told me I talked too much. I was embarrassed, so I came up with a foolproof plan to fix it: I would only speak one hundred words in a day.

I didn't make it through breakfast.

Imagine my surprise when the Lord called me to talk for a living.

Psychologists tell us there are two core fears that keep us from being vulnerable. One is the fear of rejection: *If I let you in, you'll leave.* The other is the fear of engulfment: *If I let you in, I'll disappear.* In other words, some of us are afraid we'll be abandoned, and some of us are afraid we'll be overtaken.[2]

Both are painful in their own way.

If you grew up in a home where you were trained to make sure others were comfortable, you may have come to believe that vulnerability was too much for them. You tempered your honesty to avoid rocking the boat. You learned it was your job to manage other people's moods, and vulnerability caused unnecessary waves. Maybe you got good at reading the room and keeping things light. You kept your true emotions on mute—not because you didn't have them, but because you couldn't risk what might happen if they got too loud. That's the fear of rejection.

Or maybe as a child you learned to scan the room for emotional shifts and make decisions based on what was best for other people. Don't say something that could upset them. Don't disagree if it might cause conflict. Apologize even if you don't think you did anything wrong—because it's better than living with tension. Childhood taught you it's better to be easy, low-maintenance, and pleasant rather than "too much" or "too sensitive."

Love had conditions and unwritten rules. We were told to be careful about what we shared because it reflected on our family: "Don't put your trash on the street where people can see it." The underlying message was, *If they really knew, they'd reject us.* And what our brains heard was: *Never let anyone see the truth if it isn't pretty.*

Acceptance came with invisible boundary lines, and even a toe outside those lines could result in consequences.

On the other hand, maybe you grew up in a family that felt too close—where boundaries were blurry and expectations were heavy. You were praised for being easy, self-sufficient, undemanding. You learned early that the only way to feel safe was to stay private, to keep space between yourself and others. Vulnerability felt like exposure, and connection felt like obligation. So you shut down. You kept your feelings small and your world tightly managed—not because you didn't want intimacy, but because you didn't know how to have it without losing yourself. That's the fear of being controlled.

You may have learned that cutting others off emotionally is a good way to avoid vulnerability, so you simply shut down that part of yourself. Instead of opening up, you back away by making jokes or changing the subject. You don't return texts or attend events where you might have to deal with hard conversations.

What inevitably happens is that the things we keep in the shadows fester inside us. They morph into shapes that convince us even more that they should never see the light of day. The longer we wait, the more convinced we become that revealing the truth could destroy us.

What you've seen as protective is actually prohibitive.

Our thoughts are messy. Our hearts are burdened. The weight of being unknown is more than we can bear—and yet the alternative is scarier than we can imagine.

Healthy Steps Toward Vulnerability

Let's talk through a few things to keep in mind while you work toward healthy vulnerability.

Remember what's true about you.

One of the biggest roadblocks to vulnerability is believing that the other person's response is a goal to achieve or avoid. We don't open ourselves to others so they can tell us who we are; true vulnerability always speaks from a place of already knowing who we are in God. We don't share things to tell a human story—we tell them to invite others into the holy story.

If not, you speak, and the anxiety immediately sets in. You're scanning the other person's face for any sign of judgment or rejection, and you start to shape your words around their responses. It's the absolute worst.

Instead, you can ground yourself in the reality that nothing they say or do changes how your Father in heaven sees you and speak from there. It's the only way to invite people into your life without letting them define it.

Before you open up to someone, take a moment to anchor yourself in who God says you are. Ask yourself, *Am I sharing this from a place of security in God's love, or am I desperately seeking validation?* If you're fishing for someone to tell you you're valuable, pause. Go to God first. Remind yourself, *I am His beloved daughter. Nothing this person says or doesn't say can change that.* Then share from that place of being already filled, not from a place of being empty and hoping they'll fill you.

Start small and safe.

Here's what I've discovered: Vulnerability isn't about trauma dumping or oversharing—it's about creating an atmosphere of trust through appropriate transparency. When I try to fast-track intimacy by sharing too much too soon, I'm usually operating from a place of desperation rather than security.

I challenge myself to take small risks in low-stakes situations first. I don't share my deepest struggles with an acquaintance, but I might admit I'm having a hard day. I start where it's safe and see how it goes, paying attention to both my motivations and how the other person is engaging.

Remember that transparency and vulnerability are different. Transparency is telling the truth in a way that can still maintain distance, while vulnerability is allowing someone access to the intimate parts of you that most of the world doesn't see.

Release your expectations.

I've come to realize that the more specific my expectations are for how someone should respond to my vulnerability, the more disappointed and hurt I am when they don't meet them. When I share something vulnerable and expect them to respond with exactly the right words, the right level of empathy, or the right follow-up questions, I'm setting both of us up for failure.

Before I share, I remind myself that I can't control their capacity for intimacy or their comfort level with deep conversations. Some people will lean in beautifully; others will change the subject or respond awkwardly. Instead of taking their response as a commentary on my worth, I recognize it as information about their emotional availability. I practice saying, "I shared this because I wanted to be honest, not because I needed a specific response." This frees me to be authentic without being manipulative.

Because here's the truth: People will disappoint you. They'll respond awkwardly, change the subject, or worse, use your vulnerability against you. In those moments, practice the redirect. Instead of spiraling into *I never should have shared that* or *There must be something wrong with me*, redirect to God's truth. *This person's response tells me about their capacity, not my worth. God, thank You that Your love for me never wavers, never disappoints, never runs out.*

Expect the vulnerability hangover.

By virtue of its definition, vulnerability comes at a cost. You might walk away from a conversation and immediately start regretting what you shared or obsessing over what that person might think of you now. You're queasy because you might have said too much and you don't know if you can look them in the eye the next time you're together.

This is what I call the vulnerability hangover, and it's as predictable as it is miserable. One minute you're feeling brave and connected, sharing something real with someone you trust. The next minute you're lying awake at 2 a.m. replaying every word, convinced you've ruined everything.

You start regretting what you shared, convinced you said too much, too fast. Maybe you find yourself sending funny memes to try to get back to "normal" or avoiding them entirely because facing them feels awkward. Every interaction gets filtered through your vulnerability—they seem quiet, they don't text back immediately, they cancel plans—and suddenly everything feels like evidence that they're judging your mess.

Here's what you need to know: The vulnerability hangover is not evidence that you made a mistake. It's evidence that you did something brave, and your brain is trying to protect you from future danger by making you regret it.

When this kind of regret hits, resist the urge to take back what you said or apologize for sharing. Remember why you opened up in the first place—not to get a specific response, but because authenticity is better than pretending, and connection is better than hiding. Give it time—the discomfort usually peaks within a day or two and then starts to fade. Instead of focusing on how awkward you feel, pay attention to what really happened. Sometimes the vulnerability hangover convinces us we've damaged something that was actually strengthened.

The truth is, vulnerability isn't just a relational dynamic or a psychological process—it's also spiritual warfare. Satan has a vested interest in keeping us isolated and hidden, because communal, authentic relationships are threatening to him. When we choose to be vulnerable instead of staying invisible, we are pushing back against loneliness and stepping into God's plan for us—to be known by one another and by Him.

When we do this, Jesus shifts the narrative. What was hidden and shameful is being used to point to glory, and our weaknesses are being redefined by His strength. He takes the very things that made us hide and shows a watching world that we belong to the Healer.

The vulnerability hangover is the enemy's last-ditch effort to get you back in the shadows. Don't let him win. Your openness never moves you farther away from Jesus—it moves you closer to the abundant life He designed you for.

Acting on What You Believe

Picture this: Sicily, somewhere between BC and AD.

Those of you who watch shows about four old ladies in Miami tracked with me on that one.

The Bleeding Woman's Story

For more about this woman and her story of vulnerability, see Mark 5:21-43.

Anyway, it was a normal day for Jesus as the crowds gathered around him and a high-ranking synagogue leader begged him to heal his twelve-year-old daughter. She was about to die, so it was kind of a "let's head that way now" situation.

They were heading there when Jesus abruptly stopped and asked a strange question: "Who touched me?" Someone had to be the pragmatist, especially considering they were in a wee bit of a hurry, so Peter stepped up.

"There's a pretty big crowd, Jesus. Could be anyone, and based on our time crunch, I think we should just move along."

But Jesus wasn't asking a rhetorical question—He knew someone had touched Him because He felt power leave His body. He asked again.

A woman hesitantly stepped forward; she hadn't touched Him so much as the tassel at the end of His robe. But there she was—caught. It was the worst thing that could have possibly happened. The spotlight was on her for all the wrong reasons. Worst of all, everyone else knew she shouldn't even be there. She'd been dealing with an unfortunate bout of menstrual bleeding for a dozen years and was considered unclean. She'd been to all the doctors in her network and out of it, but to no avail. She had been shunned, and by touching other people, she would make them unclean as well.

When she'd heard Jesus would be passing through, she realized she had nothing to lose. Maybe she would be healed and get her life back. What she did not imagine was that He would share her shame with everyone else.

But here's the tricky part: She was healed the instant she touched His garment, and she knew it. In that moment, she knew two things were true: She had been healed, and in order to tell the story, she would have to tell them what she had been healed of.

She had become an expert in staying invisible, and now Jesus was telling her publicly that He saw her. I don't think I'm the only one who has ever thought it would be awesome to be healed without being seen.

Just make it better without embarrassing me. Take it away without letting them judge me and send me away. Make it right, but do it where it's too dark for people to see.

That's not the way it works.

Jesus waited for her to raise her hand and confess that she was the one who touched His hem, but He didn't stop there.

He asked her to tell her story. In fact, Scripture says she told Him her whole story.

Someone grab a therapy couch—we've got an extended appointment situation.

"My sister was always mean to me growing up . . . when I was fifteen, I stole a bike . . . I'm allergic to shellfish . . ."

And let's not forget there was an innocent twelve-year-old girl who was about to die, waiting on Jesus.

But He was telling this woman it wasn't time for sugar-coating things—it was time to be vulnerable. The most beautiful testimonies come from those who have been healed not just in spite of their stories but in the midst of them.

Maybe that's what vulnerability really is: acting on the fact that we believe in the God of healing. It's evidence of exquisite faith; it's a declaration that hope lives. It is a way of saying that you believe restoration is more powerful than rejection.

I genuinely believe that Jesus delights in making our weakness strong in Him. It isn't just one more thing for Him to tolerate about us—it's the mark of a humble disciple.

But they'll call me a failure. They'll call me a loser. They'll call me a hypocrite, a laughingstock, and an embarrassment.

I'm sure the woman who touched Jesus was anticipating those names, but there was one I guarantee she wasn't expecting: daughter.

This broken, uninvited woman who was considered unclean by her community was the only person Jesus called by that name in the entirety of Scripture.

This isn't flippant language, either. In that time period, that word implied a legal adoption; it was a spoken signature on her papers.

She was healed and she was His—as are you.

Nothing in this world can change this. Not other people's opinions or responses. Not your own sense of value or your painful experiences. Nothing can shake your true identity—and it is worth celebrating. In fact, take a deep breath right now and let that settle on you.

You are healed. You are His.

What often happens is that we are so fearful of human consequences that we miss the opportunity to be more like Jesus. He invited this woman to tell her story because He knew the end of the story: His love conquers shame.

Now I want to walk a little ahead of this story into days we don't see in Scripture. I can't tell you for sure what happened to the woman in this story, but I imagine the people around her didn't point at her and laugh anymore. I doubt they called her names and reminded her of her dozen years of shame. They didn't whisper and laugh when she walked into the room, questioning the nerve she had to be among them the way they would have in the past.

How could they?

She was now known as the woman Jesus had healed. She now had a legacy that could never be taken from her. She was the beloved daughter of God, made whole in Christ.

Speaking of daughters, you should know that the twelve-year-old girl did, in fact, die before Jesus made it to her. Before you worry too much about that, you should also know that He didn't leave her that way.

Jesus has always been in the business of resurrecting what the world sees as too far gone, and those who get to see it are invited into the miracle.

Tell the story He is asking you to share from the strength

that comes from being settled as a daughter. And blessed be those who bear witness to it.

A Benediction for Those Who Go First

May you learn the power of telling your story to those who will honor it, and may you share your heart even when it's uncomfortable. I pray you find the value in letting others know the things you've tried to keep hidden. May Satan lose power when light is shed on truth.

May you encourage others to share too, and as you do, may you form bonds that can withstand the winds of life. As you lean into vulnerability, may a weight be lifted off your shoulders, and may you remember that the Lord knows everything about you. He will never leave your side, not for a moment.

11

Take All the Space You Need

You are worthy.

I think our capacity for wholeheartedness can never be greater than our willingness to be broken-hearted. It means engaging with the world from a place of vulnerability and worthiness.

BRENÉ BROWN

I don't know that I am equipped to write this chapter, least of all today.

It's not the one I was supposed to be working on, but it's the one I'm living right now, so if I'm going to tell you to go through it, I have to be willing to as well.

I'm supposed to be somewhere in an hour, but I decided not to go because I know I will feel the way I do every time I make myself show up there: like it's sixth grade and I don't know who to sit with, and I have the distinct feeling that most of the people I'm talking to are tolerating me more than liking me. I'm not exactly sure why this is the case, but all I can say is that a place that's supposed to feel like home makes me feel like a stranger trying to fit in.

Years ago, someone asked me this: "When you walk into a room, do you assume you are welcome to be there as your true self?"

For me, the answer is never.

In this particular situation, I don't think it's in my head, but the few times I have hinted at it, I feel embarrassed and self-conscious. Sometimes I think pretending it isn't the case is easier than acknowledging that it probably is, so when I'm brave enough to go, I act like everything is fine and try to make just enough small talk to fit in but not enough to stand out. Inevitably I come home and replay the conversations in my head, wondering why I'm not worthy of being there. While I write this, I'm sitting on my couch, crying. I'm not telling you this so you will feel sorry for me—I'm telling you because I want you to know that I relate to this topic on a deep level, and to a certain extent, it has been that way for years.

I just flat out don't know who I'm supposed to be in that room.

I moved back to America from Japan just before sixth grade, and it took me a while to make the transition and find my footing. I will say that even when I didn't have a lot of friends, I was the daughter of people who loved me. Home wasn't perfect, but it was safe, and I never doubted for a moment that my parents would move heaven and earth to make sure I was happy.

I can't say I doubted my worthiness as far as my family was concerned, but I quickly learned that the rest of the world didn't see me through their eyes, and it planted a seed that has grown for years: I am safe to be myself with people when I offer them what they want from me. The lie is that who I am isn't enough, but if I can figure out how to show them the version of me they prefer, I'll work my way into a place of acceptance.

Shortly after we returned to the States, my school had a science fair, and you could choose to do it with a partner or work on your own. One of the more popular girls asked me if I wanted to team up with her, and it surprised me, but I was really excited that she'd chosen me. I found out later in the day that it was a practical joke.

I went home and cried while I told my dad what had happened, and in his sweet way, he said, "Well, Angela, don't worry about that. How about you and I do it together? Maybe we could study the way rain comes off of roofs or something cool."

I have no idea why he suggested that, nor do I know why I remember that he suggested the roof thing, but I do remember having a knot in my stomach because I was equal parts embarrassed and grateful that he offered to work with me. As it turned out, Katie's partner was a dud and didn't care about the project, so she came back to me. Of course, I jumped at the opportunity because I am nothing if not proud. My dad was disappointed that we weren't going to work together, so I let him help. Katie basically wanted a free ride to avoid work, although as I recall I did go over to her house to help her with the banner.

So you won't lose sleep wondering what the project turned out to be, I will tell you: We studied the way Venus flytraps digest nutrients. We did not place.

Probably should have stuck to the roof idea.

Another stellar middle school memory involves some girls in my neighborhood inviting me over to audition to be a ballet teacher for a little school they were going to start. My mom helped me make sure I had a leotard and ballet shoes and wished me luck as she dropped me off. They had me stretch out on a bar and copy everything they did.

I honestly felt like it had gone pretty well, and I asked how long they thought it would be before I found out if I'd made it. They told me they weren't sure, so I thanked them and walked outside, slipping my plastic glasses back on. Just as the door closed behind me, I heard them roaring with laughter. There was never a ballet school—just an opportunity to humiliate me.

As you can probably tell, I still have work to do in this area. But here's what I have learned: If we want to embrace our true worth, we need to identify what's holding us back, understand why, and be reminded of the truth.

Who Are You When No One Is Watching?

Do you know who you are when you walk into a room, or do you become whoever you think the room needs you to be?

I wish I could sit with you and ask you who you are when no one is watching. Not what you do or how you perform or what roles you fill, but who you are in the quiet moments when the world isn't asking anything of you. I wonder if you would say that you are most yourself when you serve others, make them happy, back down when you need to, stand up when you have to, or make them proud through accomplishments. As believers, we know the true story: We are beloved children of God, created in His image, chosen and known.

And yet we can't dismiss the fact that the world wants us to build our identity everywhere else.

Some people are solid in their identity—they know who they are regardless of context. They don't shift and shape themselves based on who's watching. They carry the same sense of self from room to room, relationship to relationship.

For others, identity feels fluid and fragmented—they become different versions of themselves depending on who they're with and what they think is expected of them. They've learned to read the room and adapt, to perform whatever version of themselves seems safest or most useful in the moment.

The difference isn't confidence or social skills—it's whether you believe you have permission to be the same person everywhere or whether you've learned that survival requires constant adaptation to external expectations.

People who feel permission to be consistent no matter the context operate from a foundation of secure identity. They believe they belong simply because they exist, and they don't see their authentic self as something that needs justification.

People who feel they must constantly adapt operate from fractured identity—they believe their true self is contingent on context, that who they really are might not be acceptable, so they live with constant low-level anxiety about which version of themselves to present.

This isn't about arrogance versus humility. Someone can be deeply humble and still carry the same sense of self everywhere.

Do you assume that the invitation is genuine or that you were invited out of obligation? Do you assume that people want to hear what you have to say or that you should keep quiet? Do you assume that you can be yourself or that you need to become someone else to fit in?

Your answer to the identity question shapes everything: how you enter rooms, navigate relationships, respond to conflict, handle success and failure. It's the lens you use to decide which version of yourself to present in every social interaction.

As kids, our brains weren't sophisticated enough to separate rejection from identity, so the two bled together. When a child experiences rejection—not being picked for a team, being laughed at during a presentation, being excluded from a birthday party, or targeted by a cruel "joke"—their developing brain draws the wrong conclusion. Instead of thinking, *That person was unkind* or *That situation was unfair*, they think, *Who I am isn't safe here.*

This creates the identity wound—not the rejection itself, but the story you tell yourself about whether your true self is acceptable. Your brain tries to make sense of it with a narrative that says who you really are isn't wanted, doesn't fit—that you need to become someone else to belong.

When you're braced for identity rejection, you're unable to be present as yourself. The assumption that who you really are isn't welcome makes genuine connection difficult—you perform instead of simply being yourself. You manage your persona instead of offering your authentic self.

Remembering Your True Identity

If you find yourself wrestling with which identity to show up with in any given situation, it isn't easy to unlearn these lessons, but it's never too late.

The Identity Check: Before entering a situation, ask yourself, *Who am I here?* If the answer is different from who you are at home or with your closest friend, pause. You don't have to perform a different version of yourself to belong.

The Authentic Contribution: Instead of asking, *What do they want from me?* Ask, *What do I have to offer as myself?* Your genuine personality, perspective, and presence are the contribution—not some curated version you think other people would prefer.

Permission to Be Consistent: You don't have to become more outgoing for extroverts or more serious for formal settings. Adapting your behavior is different from changing your identity. You can be appropriately respectful while remaining fundamentally yourself.

The Identity Anchor: Instead of waiting to feel safe to be yourself, start being yourself and let the safety catch up. Speak in your natural voice, share your actual thoughts, exist authentically in the space. Identity is often discovered through consistency, not performance.

There will be days when all the tools in the world feel too heavy to pick up. Days when showing up as yourself feels impossible and when staying true to your identity seems like pretending. On those days, you don't need more strategies—you need permission.

Permission to take up space: You don't have to shrink yourself to make others comfortable. Your presence is not an imposition. You were created to occupy space in this world—stop apologizing for existing fully.

Permission to be imperfect: Your identity isn't contingent on your performance. You can mess up and still be yourself. Mistakes don't disqualify you from authenticity—they qualify you for grace.

Your identity isn't something you achieve—it's something you remember.

What would your life look like if you truly walked in the identity that Jesus has bestowed upon you through His wild love? You may find that you don't need to perform anymore, and when that happens, the rest of the world takes note.

The One You've Been Waiting For

The easiest way to avoid shame in relationships is to not let anyone get close enough to you to see the things you're embarrassed about. One of the most tender stories in all of the New Testament features a woman who had structured her days around avoiding shame. But a single encounter changed her life.

The Woman at the Well's Story

For more about the Samaritan woman and how she discovered her true identity, see John 4:1-42.

She came to gather water every day when it was sweltering hot because she knew the other women wouldn't be there at that time. She was looked down on and carried a great deal of shame; I imagine it was easier to stay away than to feel the eyes of people judging her.

One day, there was a Man sitting by the well, and He asked her to draw water for Him. There were a lot of reasons why this was countercultural, and she wasn't afraid to point them out. When you read the story, you can sense her defensiveness and immediate assumption that this was somehow a trick or a setup.

She was a woman (strike one), a Samaritan (next strike—Jews didn't interact with Samaritans), and a known sinner (and you're out). Asking for water had to come with some strings, because they both knew who she was and that she wasn't acceptable to serve Him.

This next part is spectacular, but I fear it's sometimes missed. Scripture says that in response, Jesus replied, "If you knew who was asking you for water, you would have asked Him for living water."

He wasn't asking her to serve Him. He was telling her that if she asked, *He* would serve *her*. This was an absurd proposition, for a number of reasons—and certainly would never have crossed her mind.

He had, in a handful of words, flipped the entire script of humanity.

She didn't yet understand that this conversation was about more than water, and she was focused on the logistics. He didn't even have a jar—how on earth was He going to get water? The well was too deep, and she reminded Him of it.

He explained that He was talking about something much more beautiful: living water.

Then He told her to get her husband and come back, and she told Him the truth without telling Him the whole truth: "I don't have a husband."

And here we go. She thought she was going to get off on a technicality, but Jesus wasn't having it.

"You're right! You don't have a husband. You've had five, and the man you are with now is not your husband."

What's beautiful is that nothing in the text suggests He was condemning her, nor did it seem that He was holding it over her head. She was shocked, and she told Him that one day a Messiah was coming and His name would be Christ. He would explain everything, and they were waiting for Him.

Jesus spoke, and the power of God spilled out:

"I am He. I'm the One you've been waiting for all these years. I know exactly who you are and how much you have believed what the world says about you, but I see something else, and it is only My opinion that matters."

How could anyone know everything about her and seek her out—not to shame her, but to tell her who she really is?

Not only was she a woman who was not a Jew, but she was the first non-Jewish woman we have record of Jesus speaking to. He could not have chosen a more unlikely candidate for redemption.

It is also Jesus' longest one-on-one conversation recorded in the entirety of the Bible, and it's with a woman who was considered undeniably worthless by society's standards.

She was so overwhelmed by His words that she ran away from the well, leaving her jar behind. I imagine she left many other things behind that day, as we often do when we realize the Messiah has come.

The woman didn't immediately run back to the place where she was living in sin; she ran directly into the town that held everyone who judged her. The only thing louder than their accusations was her testimony, and she knew it.

Lean in to the text. I am convinced that some of the greatest moments in Scripture are tucked away in the details.

She didn't run to tell them that she was clean. She didn't say she had been redeemed. She didn't justify herself or try to convince them that she was no longer who she was. In fact, she did exactly the opposite: She told them that she believed

He was the Messiah—because He knew the truth of who she was.

The very thing that brought her to the well in the heat of the day was what brought the truth to the people who had forced her to be there at that time.

"Come, see a man who told me everything I ever did," she proclaimed to the very people who had whispered about her for years. She didn't say, "Come see a man who has made me clean" or "Come see a man who has given me a fresh start." She said, "Come see a man who knows all my secrets—and still calls me His own."

This is the identity paradox: Our greatest shame becomes our most powerful witness when we understand that we are fully known and fully loved for who we really are.

The woman could have tried to rehabilitate her image. She could have spent years slowly proving she had changed, carefully managing her reputation, hoping that eventually people would forget her past. Instead, she made her past the centerpiece of her testimony—not because she was proud of it, but because Jesus' response to it proved who He was.

When we truly grasp that Jesus knows everything about us and still calls us His own, we stop needing to perform. We realize that our testimony isn't about who we've become but about who He says we've always been. We realize that our testimony isn't about how good we've become but about how good He is to the broken.

When we stop trying to earn our way, an incredible thing

happens: Our scars become our credentials, our failures become our qualifications to speak about grace, and our deepest shame becomes the very thing that points others to the One who calls us by name.

Getting a New Name

You may recall that we started this journey with a man who spent his entire life pretending and eventually became the father of the tribes of Israel. From his lineage would come the Messiah who would walk on water, heal the bleeding woman, and sit beside the woman at this well.

I am He.

This was not about the water the earth provides; it was the living water that gives you a new name.

It was no coincidence that the Messiah chose a well that had a history of its own.

Centuries before this moment, the land was owned by Jacob, hence the name: Jacob's well.

What is your name?

I am Jacob, the deceiver. I am Jacob, the usurper. The pretender. The performer. But I will not let You go until You bless me, because I believe You can.

Jacob's Story, Part 2

For more about Jacob and how he discovered his true identity, see Genesis 32:22-32.

We wrestle against everything the world says we are, but we do so on hallowed ground.

The threads that have woven through every chapter of this book converge here at this ancient well: Our desperate attempts to control our image, our exhaustion from constant comparison, our fear of conflict and vulnerability, our hurried pursuit of approval, our perfectionistic striving—all of it has been a journey to this moment, when Jesus sits and offers the living water we've been searching for all along.

We walk dusty trails following the Messiah, eventually coming to believe that we are more than what others say we are. We offer our weakness, our brokenness, our shame, our longings, and our hope because we believe that our stories are held in the Book of Life and that our testimonies hold out hope to a watching world.

He offers the living water that satisfies, brought to the surface by the Savior who knows everything about you.

Your worth was settled before you took your first breath. Your belonging was secured before you ever worried about where to sit. Your identity was established before you ever felt the need to prove yourself worthy of love.

By now you know that those who limp can also walk on water, and those with a shady past can be redeemed. Those who have been condemned can be healed, and those who have sinned can be restored.

The One who loves you has called you daughter, and no other name is louder.

Come, all who are weary.

Come, receive living water, because nothing else will satisfy.

Come as you are, all you sinners and saints; come to Jacob's well.

Your Father is offering you the water of life from deep within the well, and I pray that today and every day after will find you brave enough to accept it.

A Benediction for Those Who Doubt Their Worth

May you never forget your true worth. When you do forget, may the Lord speak truth over you and remind you that you were made in His perfect image. When the world tries to tell you who you are, may you remember that the Lord has already declared the truth: You are His. You don't have anything to prove. You don't have to perform. You don't have to pretend.

May the God of heaven and earth speak His words of love over you now and every moment of the days to come.

CONCLUSION

Where the Shallows Meet the Depth

Every chapter of this book has led you to the place you are now—to the place where the shallows meet the depth. This isn't a place for you to act like you have it all together; it's the place where you start admitting you never will. You've met characters from Scripture who walked the line between the surface and the sacred, and you've learned that you can be brave and honest in a world that doesn't always encourage it.

Comparison can't complete us.

Hurry won't heal our hearts.

Pretending will never replace being present.

We have to learn to be slow in a world that demands speed and forgiving when others keep records of wrong.

We have to fight to be vulnerable when we want to hide and to be honest even when the truth hurts.

I didn't write this book because I have learned to do all these things perfectly; I wrote it because, like you, I long to keep walking in that direction. The world will never tell us that we're enough, and it's time to stop asking it to.

Being still can simply be taking a breath as you walk into a room, and being brave can mean setting your phone aside when you'd rather cling to a sense of control. None of this has to be drastic or overnight—it's a lifelong pilgrimage that unfolds in thousands of small obediences.

I pray that you will unlearn the patterns that have held you captive and that you will steady your soul in Jesus.

Above all, I pray that you will remember you are beloved, worthy, and treasured, even when you feel misplaced, forgotten, and afraid. Never, not for one moment, has that been the case, and it never will be.

I pray that you will run from this place and tell the world of the Man you met—the One who knows all about you and offered you the water of heaven.

I pray that the waves that have scared you in the past will become your testimony and that you will have a life that overflows with hope.

I pray that when you're tempted to go back to shore, you will fight the current and remember where your true home is.

You, beloved, were born to live in the deep.

Acknowledgments

I want to start by thanking my incredible team at Tyndale. It's been a while since I wrote and even longer since I believed in my writing—you redeemed all of it and more. I will never stop being grateful for you and the way you welcomed me and brought me back to life.

For Karen and Curtis, who have stuck with me, fought for me, and believed in me for what . . . a dozen years? You are excellent at your jobs, but more than that, you are the kind of friends people would be honored to have. You've been inside my real life and have given me the honor of being inside yours. Curtis, one question: Do you like this book?

For my co-teachers at school, who stayed hours after school to pray for me when I was on Zoom calls with publishers, kept me fed because they knew I would forget lunch, cried with me when I felt defeated, and celebrated my wins as their own—I am certain I never would have been able to do this without you. I treasure you deeply and thank God for the years we've had together and the ones to come.

For Joy, who walked with me while pounding her own keyboard. We never got as much work done together as we should have, and I'm grateful for it. This book is better because of your insights, thoughtfulness, and wild imagination. Your name isn't featured on the pages, but a good bit of your wisdom is—thank you for being a sounding board and cheerleader.

For Jess, who has loved me for so many years that she can forgive me for falling off the radar. I will never stop thanking God for your friendship. I love you deeply and am more proud of you than you will ever know.

For my mom, who teaches me every day that miracles are possible. I will never be able to tell you how proud I am of you and how dearly I love you. You are the joy of every room, and you love purely and faithfully. I have never doubted how proud you are of me, and I will never forget how many times you asked me how this book was coming along. You are a treasure to me, and I am so grateful to be your daughter.

For Jenn, who I will never stop thanking God for. You're the only one who understands what this life has handed us—from the magic to the mourning. You are a teammate, a friend, and the best sisto a girl could ask for. I'm crying as I write these words, knowing that you can see all the words I can't fit. I love you so much, J.

For Todd, Ellie, Abby, Kate, and Charlotte—I want you to know that I see the sacrifices you made while I got my doctorate and wrote these words. You were selfless, attentive, forgiving, and encouraging with every step, and I don't know how to thank you. You believe in me so much that I can't help but trust you, and you make Jesus more real to me every day. There is nothing more I could have asked for in this life than our precious family, and I will never take it for granted. You are the reason acknowledgments are so hard for me to write, because certain things can never be explained, even by a writer. I pray you know them in spite of that and never doubt them for a moment.

For Dad—nothing makes me prouder than being your daughter, even when you're not here for me to tell you so. I know that somehow, in some way, you were with me at that stoplight while I drove your car and told the Lord I was giving up on Him because He took you from me. *Pick up your pen and write, Angela. Tell them everything, because it's all true.* Well, I did it, Dad; I guess you always knew I would. I have a new cap and gown to show you one day—you always knew I would do that too. I don't know exactly how to live without you here, but I'm trying. I love you forever, Dad.

Notes

CHAPTER 1: TAKING OFF THE MASK

1. Abigail Gómez-Morales, "Impostor Phenomenon: A Concept Analysis," *Nursing Science Quarterly* 34, no. 3 (2021): 309–315, https://pubmed.ncbi.nlm.nih.gov/34212809/.
2. David G. Benner, *The Gift of Being Yourself: The Sacred Call to Self-Discovery* (InterVarsity Press, expanded edition 2015), 83.
3. Virginia Satir, *The New Peoplemaking* (Science and Behavior Books, 1988).

CHAPTER 2: YOU WON'T MISS A THING

1. Katharina Schäfer and Tuomas Eerola, "How Listening to Music and Engagement with Other Media Provide a Sense of Belonging: An Exploratory Study of Social Surrogacy," *Psychology of Music* 48, no. 2 (2018): 232–251, https://journals.sagepub.com/doi/abs/10.1177/0305735618795036.

CHAPTER 3: MORE THAN A GUEST IN SOMEONE ELSE'S STORY

1. Suzanne Degges-White, "The Chameleon Effect: Why We Mirror Friends and Lovers," *Psychology Today*, December 21, 2023, https://www.psychologytoday.com/us/blog/lifetime-connections/202312/the-chameleon-effect-why-we-mirror-friends-and-lovers#:~:text=Key%20points,extent%20without%20even%20realizing%20it.
2. Dan P. McAdams, "Narrative Identity," in *Handbook of Identity Theory and Research*, ed. Seth J. Schwartz et al. (Springer, 2011), 99–115.

CHAPTER 5: NOTHING TO PROVE

1. Kendra Cherry, "What Is a Schema in Psychology?" Verywell Mind, October 17, 2025, https://www.verywellmind.com/what-is-a-schema-2795873#:~:text=In%20psychology%2C%20a%20schema%20is,memories%20of%20our%20unique%20experiences.

2. Paul L. Hewitt and Gordon L. Flett, "Perfectionism in the Self and Social Contexts: Conceptualization, Assessment, and Association with Psychopathology, *Journal of Personality and Social Psychology* 60, no. 3 (1991): 456–470, https://doi.org/10.1037/0022-3514.60.3.456.
3. "Exposure with Response Prevention (ERP)," Sheppard Pratt, accessed November 22, 2025, https://www.sheppardpratt.org/knowledge-center/treatment/exposure-with-response-prevention-erp.

CHAPTER 8: MADE FOR CONNECTION

1. Jeffrey A. Hall, "How Many Hours Does It Take to Make a Friend?" *Journal of Social and Personal Relationships* 36, no. 4 (2018): 1278–1296, https://doi.org/10.1177/0265407518761225.

CHAPTER 9: A GOOD KIND OF HURT

1. Timothy D. Wilson and Daniel T. Gilbert, "Affective Forecasting: Knowing What to Want," *Current Directions in Psychological Science* 14, no. 3 (2005): 131–134, https://doi.org/10.1111/j.0963-7214.2005.00355.x.
2. Amie M. Gordon, "Be Careful What You Focus On," *Psychology Today*, March 5, 2018, https://www.psychologytoday.com/us/blog/between-you-and-me/201803/be-careful-what-you-focus.

CHAPTER 10: THE TENDER PLACES OF YOUR SOUL

1. Charlotte Nickerson, "Looking-Glass Self: Theory, Definition & Examples," Simply Psychology, September 22, 2023, https://www.simplypsychology.org/charles-cooleys-looking-glass-self.html.
2. Mara Hirschfeld, "Fear of Engulfment: How to Maintain Your Sense of Self in Relationships," Holding Hope Marriage and Family Therapy, June 13, 2024, https://holdinghopemft.com/fear-of-engulfment-how-to-maintain-your-sense-of-self-in-relationships/.

About the Author

Angie Smith is a bestselling author, Bible teacher, and speaker with a PhD in developmental psychology. Her works include the popular Bible studies *Seamless* and *Matchless*, as well as the books *Chasing God* and *What Women Fear*. She loves helping people explore the deeper layers of their faith and emotional life. Known for her blend of honesty, humor, and heartfelt storytelling, she weaves together psychological insight and biblical truth in ways that feel both accessible and transformative. Angie has walked alongside thousands of readers as they move from surface-level survival into wholehearted, grounded living with God. When she's not writing, she's teaching middle school English and spending time with her husband and four daughters in Franklin, Tennessee.